Discovering Friendly and Fraternal Societies:
Their Badges and Regalia

Victoria Solt Dennis

A Shire book

Cover: *A collection of friendly and fraternal artefacts from the eighteenth, nineteenth and twentieth centuries.*

ACKNOWLEDGEMENTS

All images are copyright of, and reproduced with the permission of, the Library and Museum of Freemasonry.

The author would like to thank: the Library and Museum of Freemasonry and especially its curatorial staff, Mark Dennis and Fay Newman, for their assistance with the research for this book; the Supreme Grand Chapter of England for its sponsorship of initial research; Andy Durr; Pauline Scott; and Professor Andrew Prescott at the Centre for Research into Freemasonry at Sheffield University; Dr Dan Weinbren and the Friendly Societies Research Group at the Open University for their comments and advice; and all those millions of members of friendly and fraternal societies who chose to mark their membership with the regalia and badges that are the subject of this book.

British Library Cataloguing in Publication Data: Dennis, Victoria Solt. Discovering friendly and fraternal societies: their badges and regalia. – (Discovering series; no. 295) 1. Friendly societies – Great Britain – Insignia 2. Friendly societies – Great Britain – History I. Title 334.7'0941. ISBN-10: 0 7478 0628 4.

Published in 2005 by Shire Publications Ltd, Cromwell House, Church Street, Princes Risborough, Buckinghamshire HP27 9AA, UK. (Website: www.shirebooks.co.uk) Copyright © 2005 by Victoria Solt Dennis. First published 2005. Number 295 in the Discovering series. ISBN 0 7478 0628 4.

Printed in Malta by Gutenberg Press Limited, Gudja Road, Tarxien PLA 19, Malta.

Contents

History of friendly and fraternal societies 4
Friendly society artefacts 29
Symbolism used on the artefacts of friendly and fraternal societies . 50
The Freemasons 57
The Royal Antediluvian Order of Buffaloes 70
The Knights of the Golden Horn 77
The Free Gardeners 81
The Oddfellows 90
The Druids 101
The Ancient Order of Foresters 114
The Ancient Order of Loyal Shepherds 124
The Loyal Order of Ancient Shepherds 126
The 'Friends' 131
The temperance orders 142
Postscript 155
Further reading 156
Research resources 157
Places to visit 157
Index 158

History of friendly and fraternal societies

The term 'friendly society' has been used since at least the middle of the seventeenth century with the specific meaning of a mutual savings society, all of whose members paid a subscription into a common fund from which they were entitled to claim for sickness, burial costs and so on, and this is the meaning it generally has today. However, the phrase is not as simple as all that since some eighteenth-century societies of a purely social nature also called themselves 'friendly societies', meaning simply that the object of the society was friendship and sociability; and many of the members of mutual savings societies felt that sociable friendship was also one of the important purposes of their society, in some ways as important as the financial aspect. We now make a distinction between 'friendly societies' and 'fraternal societies' (the latter being societies from which the element of mutual saving is absent), but this distinction would not necessarily have been clear to the members of such societies in the seventeenth and eighteenth centuries, and all these societies have many aspects in common.

The concept of the mutual benefit society is probably as old as urban civilisation. In classical Greece and Rome members of specific trades – artisans, soldiers, even gladiators – would form clubs to which they would subscribe, and from which they could count on receiving benefits in times of need. Funeral costs were perhaps the commonest benefit subscribed for; it seems that providing for one's funeral has always been considered important, and some such clubs covered these and nothing else. Other clubs offered sickness benefit, and pensions for widows and orphans.

In the Middle Ages in Europe these needs were catered for by the guilds, which typically had a charitable fund for infirm members and members' dependants. Medieval guilds are often thought of as bodies set up to regulate craft trades, and indeed many guilds were craft-based, but many were lay religious fraternities, taking members from a variety of occupations. Whether craft-based or not, the medieval guild or fraternity was a highly social body. As the name 'fraternity' implies, it felt itself to be a symbolic family; fellow members were often called 'brothers' or 'sisters' (it was quite normal for guilds to have women members) and care was taken to foster a feeling of relationship. Guilds held collective religious observances, feasts and public processions, and members had a duty not merely to pay their dues but to attend such events, and fellow members' funerals.

Mutual benefit clubs are recorded in England from the mid seventeenth century. The author Daniel Defoe described them in 1697 and suggested the creation of a nationwide friendly society that all working people would be obliged to join in order to provide for themselves in times of sickness or unemployment and thus take the strain off the parish authorities, which were responsible for Poor Relief. (In effect Defoe had invented the concept of National Insurance more than two centuries before it was adopted by Lloyd George's government.) Nothing came of Defoe's idea, but a number of economic and political thinkers noted the phenomenon and discussed ways in which mutual benefit societies might be encouraged in order to induce the working classes to practise self-help. This impulse led eventually to the Rose Act of 1793, which gave legal recognition to friendly societies. Societies could

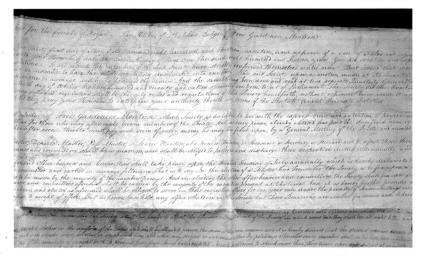

The rules and regulations of the St John's Lodge of Free Gardeners, Montrose, written on parchment and presented to a magistrate in 1820 for registration under the Rose Act.

register under the Act by enrolling their rules with a Justice of the Peace, and thus acquire legal status as corporate bodies (which gave them the right to recover debts or sue for stolen funds) and exemption from some duties such as the stamp tax on paper, which was quite a serious expense at the time. But many friendly societies, suspicious of governmental interference and unwilling to submit their rules for approval by a magistrate (who had the right to make them change rules he thought improper) did not enrol, and the Act created no means to force them to do so.

Exactly how the friendly societies evolved from the medieval fraternities is not clear. Some historians feel that the mutual benefit societies formed by French Huguenot refugees in London, such as the Society of Parisians, dating from 1687, had an influence on their development. Tantalisingly, the writers who mentioned friendly society activity in seventeenth- and eighteenth-century England were generally more interested in the financial than in the social aspects of the societies. We know that such clubs collected dues from their members, who in turn were entitled to claim a range of benefits; these typically included sickness benefits, doctors' fees, unemployment benefits, funeral expenses and widows' pensions. In addition they typically had regular social meetings and an annual feast, which like medieval guild feasts very often included a religious element; the members would go to church in procession for a service and sermon, before their festive meal. Attendance at fellow members' funerals was also normally a duty. What we do not know is whether this early friendly society activity also normally included such things as special clothing or regalia, ritual initiations and esoteric 'mysteries' as a direct inheritance from the medieval guild tradition, or if these aspects were re-imported later under the influence of Freemasonry and other middle- and upper-class social groups.

In the later seventeenth century men of the middle and upper classes in Britain began to take an interest in joining traditional trade-based societies. This happened in Scotland, where gentlemen joined fraternities of master gardeners, and most famously and importantly in England, where they joined lodges of stonemasons.

5

Certain of the medieval crafts, most notably stonemasonry, had always been peripatetic trades, in which skilled men would have to travel from place to place to find work. The guilds of such trades, unlike static trades such as butchery and bakery (which were usually localised and often refused to admit craftsmen from elsewhere to membership), had to be nationwide in character in order to provide support for their members as they moved across the country. Lodges were set up where members could work and meet fellow craftsmen. Guild members arriving in a new place had to be able to produce evidence of their craft membership, so a system of passwords and signs of recognition evolved.

It was this 'craft lodge' tradition of stonemasonry that seventeenth-century intellectuals adopted. Although it was a startling idea at the time to take up the dress and social activities of their social 'inferiors', it proved to have enormous advantages. As members of a fraternity, all Masons were equal inside the lodge; this enabled conversations and relationships between people who in normal social circumstances would have been separated by differences in rank. Because Masonic society was quite separate from ordinary social life it was possible for people to meet whose religious or political differences would normally create a gulf between them. Everything said or done in the lodge was secret, which made it safe to discuss radical new ideas. All this was an extremely creative new means of sociability, and Freemasonry became one of the engines of the eighteenth-century Enlightenment. A remarkably high proportion of the scholars, scientists and artists of that era were active Freemasons, and the first great British scientific institution, the Royal Society, was the creation of London Freemasons. Some social advances can be directly attributed to Freemasonry; for example, the acceptance of Jews in 'polite society' in the early nineteenth century largely resulted from the influence of the sons of George III, almost all of whom were keen Freemasons and who had made Jewish friends through Freemasonry at a time when they could not have met Jews socially in any other context.

The 'craft lodge' model proved flexible enough to be adapted to different needs and aims; it was replicated by many different fraternal societies in the eighteenth century and had a strong influence on the friendly societies. The basic features of such a society were quite consistent. A basic metaphor or 'foundation legend' would give the society its nomenclature and furnish it with symbols to decorate its regalia and a metaphor to expound moral teaching; typically this legend would claim extremely ancient origins for the society. Candidates for membership would be put through an initiation ceremony, typically including blindfolding, some form of 'ordeal' or fright, and an oath of secrecy concerning the order's affairs. Some societies, as in Freemasonry, had a hierarchical system of degrees of membership. Initiated members would identify themselves to each other with passwords, special handshakes ('grips') and gestures ('signs'). Lodges would meet regularly, and the meeting would include both a ritual and social eating and drinking. Each lodge would govern itself but, as lodges multiplied, increasingly they would create a Grand Lodge to which all owed obedience. Typically there would be a charitable fund for distressed members and their dependants. Some societies held public processions, which could be very elaborate, such as that of the Royal Grand Order of Jerusalem Sols in London in August 1787, which included 130 coaches.

A typical example of such a society is the Most Ancient and Honourable Society of Bucks, which flourished between the 1770s and the 1820s. An account of the society published in 1770, evidently by a member, includes a long mock-scholarly description of how the society was founded by Nimrod,

Collar of the Jerusalem Sols: blue silk decorated with figured gold lace. The jewel at the centre is a painted enamel scene of the Theological Virtues surrounded by paste jewels; the plaque at the bottom reads 'James T Reed, Recorder of the Royal Grand Arch Constitutional Sols Lodge, Instituted Novr. 23 1785'. The collar buttons at the back.

Right: *Jewel of the Jerusalem Sols, probably intended to be worn suspended from a collar. The enamel scene shows an enthroned Hebrew king; the surround is paste.*

the 'mighty hunter' of the Old Testament, and modelled on Nimrod's government of the empire of the Assyrians. (Taken literally, this would imply that the Order of Bucks was more ancient than that of the Freemasons, who claimed to date merely from the building of King Solomon's temple; this may

Jewels of the Society of Bucks, dated between 1773 and 1819: paste with painted enamel roundels under glass. The star-shaped jewels imitate the breast jewels of orders of chivalry; the key-shaped jewel is probably the treasurer's badge. The jewel in the shape of a feather plume and crescent is a hat ornament; the 'plumes' are designed to tremble in movement like real feathers. The whole jewel is reminiscent of the famous 'chelengk' hat ornament presented by the Sultan of Turkey to Admiral Nelson after the Battle of the Nile and may be a deliberate allusion to it.

have been a deliberate claim to seniority on the part of the Bucks.) Extensive regulations are given for the appointment of officers, foundation of new lodges, and payment of subscriptions to the benevolent fund. Moral exhortations follow, in favour of virtue and brotherly love and against drunkenness and taking the Lord's name in vain. The author makes the (presumably) tongue-in-cheek claim that 'The greatest monarchs in all ages, as well of Asia and Africa as of Europe, have been encouragers of our noble order, and many of them have presided as grands over the Bucks in their respective dominions'. However, after all this solemn and virtuous discourse the book ends with a selection of hunting and drinking songs – and the Bucks were noted at the time for rowdy and drunken behaviour. Their members must all have been fairly well off as their surviving jewels are of very high quality, with fine enamel and paste work. Their main symbol was naturally a buck or stag, and their mottoes included 'UNANIMITY IS THE STRENGTH OF SOCIETY', 'FREEDOM WITH INNOCENCE', 'INDUSTRY PRODUCETH WEALTH' and 'BE MERRY AND WISE'.

Lodge-based societies covered all kinds of activity and interest: there were debating societies, such as the Cogers; political groupings like the Knights of the Brush, supporters of Charles James Fox; purely sociable groups like the Codheads and the Free and Easy under the Rose; and facetious groups such as the Most Ancient, Honourable and Venerable Society of Adams, a social society of the mid eighteenth century, whose first rule was that 'no young man under seventy years of age should be admitted as a member'! Socially minded men could join as many such groups as they liked; there does not seem to have been any notion of competition between the societies, or any feeling that membership of one society ruled out that of all others.

This proliferation of societies led to a good deal of social mixing. In a list dated 1796 of the Wakefield Chapter of the Gregorians, a fraternal society with a reputation for jollity and convivial mirth that stopped short of the riotous behaviour of the Bucks, the members' occupations range from a grocer, a clerk and a plumber to a doctor of divinity, a lieutenant-general and a captain in the Navy. There was also an innkeeper, which was quite usual as most societies found it a good idea to enrol the landlord of the inn at which they met into their brotherhood.

Eighteenth-century England was full of social activity of this kind until a series of political shocks threw the government and the establishment into a panic. The French Revolution in 1789 was greeted with great approval by many Englishmen of radical leanings, many of whom joined the London Corresponding Society to promote revolution in Britain also. When the new French Republic declared war and threatened an invasion of Britain in the late 1790s it seemed possible that such an invasion would actually receive widespread support and assistance from British radicals, and working-class and middle-class societies immediately became suspect. This fear was heightened by the uprising in Ireland in 1798 (with French military support) of the Society of United Irishmen, which had been founded in 1791 to promote Catholic emancipation and parliamentary reform, and which was organised along similar lines to the fraternal societies, with oaths and passwords.

The response of the government was the Unlawful Oaths Act of 1797, which outlawed societies that administered oaths of secrecy, and the Unlawful Societies Act of 1799, which repeated the ban on such oaths and also outlawed any organisations that held closed meetings and were organised into branches with national committees. Freemasonry was specifically exempted from the

Opposite page and above: Silver jewels of the Society of Gregorians, not dated or hallmarked but known to be late-eighteenth to early-nineteenth-century. They were probably designed to be worn suspended from a collar or collarette. Several are the jewels of lodge officers, with the title engraved on the reverse. Three have the emblem of the society on the obverse; one has the emblem engraved on the reverse and a mythological scene on the obverse.

Act, thanks to strenuous lobbying on the part of the royal dukes and other aristocrats who belonged to the Freemasons, on condition that every lodge register with a local magistrate and supply him with a list of its members. (This condition was only rescinded in 1967.) Other societies tried to get exemption; the Gregorians subscribed £80 17s towards 'the support of Government' in 1798 in the hope of being exempted as well, but to no avail. As a result of this Act Freemasonry, which earlier had been such a hotbed of new ideas, abjured all political activity and began to distance itself deliberately from other societies. For a while the 'craft lodge' model of sociability continued in use for gentlemen but, increasingly, apart from Freemasonry the gentlemen's club

Jewel of the Knights of Salamanca Lodge, of parcel-gilt silver. There has never been a Masonic lodge by this name; it may have been a one-off creation by officers who had fought in the Battle of Salamanca in 1812 to perpetuate their comradeship.

Jewel of the Past Noble Grand of the Lodge of Loyal Britons, 1812, reverse and obverse. It is not known what order, if any, this lodge belonged to. In the aftermath of the French Revolution and the Irish rising of 1798 many societies found it politic to add 'Loyal' to their title to emphasise that they had no subversive intent.

replaced the lodge-based society as the typical site of upper-class gentlemen's social activity. Existing genteel lodge societies, which in any case had either to alter their ceremonies radically or risk prosecution, faded out – the Gregorians around 1807, the Bucks in the 1820s. Almost the only other survivor of the elite lodge-based societies of the eighteenth century is the Friendly Brothers of St Patrick, which had been formed in Ireland in the first half of the eighteenth

century to combat duelling, which was alarmingly prevalent in Ireland at that time. The Friendly Brothers' lodges were called 'knots', symbolising the 'knot of friendship' that joined the members together. They had a strong following in the army; military lodges were called 'marching knots'. The Friendly Brothers still have their headquarters in Dublin and have 'marching knots' in the British Army.

Societies of all kinds were thrown into crisis by this legislation, which criminalised their initiations and oaths of secrecy. Many groups split, one part of the

Collarette of the Friendly Brothers of St Patrick. The white marks on the ribbon are metal polish stains.

Collar of the United Patriots Friendly Society, post-1911. This society was founded in 1842 by adherents of the Chartist reform movement, which was deeply involved in the political upheavals of the 1830s.

society bowdlerising its oaths and rituals to remain lawful, and the other part carrying on regardless of the law. A breach was created between the American fraternal societies, which, not being affected by this legislation, continued to develop and indeed to elaborate their oaths and rituals, and the British ones.

Although the Unlawful Societies Act was not repealed until 1967, as the threat of revolution and French invasion receded the government relaxed its vigilance and middle-class fraternal groups were allowed to carry on, and indeed some new societies such as the Royal Antediluvian Order of Buffaloes were founded, unhindered though technically illegal.

The situation for working-class societies was very different. The Rose Act of 1793 had been passed to legitimise and encourage friendly societies, provided that they conformed with the government's fairly narrow view of how a friendly society should be organised. At about the same time almost every other kind of working-class organisation had been outlawed, by the Unlawful Oaths and Unlawful Societies Acts, and a series of 'Combination Acts' in force between 1799 and 1824 that outlawed trade-union activity, specifically any association to improve wages or working conditions. It was not easy to distinguish a trade-based benefit society from a trade union, since much of what they did was very similar. Mutual support between members was a vital concern of both, and it must often have been difficult for a trade-based friendly society not to engage in trade-union style activities – after all, could anyone expect their members not to discuss their wages and working conditions when they met together, or refrain from discussing ways in which they might work to improve them?

'By hammer and hand, All arts do stand' – a trade-union or a friendly-society apron?

Moreover, early trade unions used ritual initiations, systems of symbolic teaching and oaths of secrecy just like those of the friendly societies to bind their members together and protect them against informers. This custom survived longer in the trade-union movement than many people realise; aprons, sashes and other regalia were worn in many unions throughout the nineteenth century, and some unions were still practising blindfold initiations into the mid twentieth. Some trade unions called themselves 'friendly societies' as a deliberate cover for their real activity – the Tolpuddle Martyrs were sentenced under the Unlawful Societies Act in 1834 for having set up a body called an Agricultural Friendly Society, for which they held an initiation in typical friendly-society form with blindfolds, oaths and an 'emblem of mortality' – a transparency of a skeleton. The Tolpuddle case caused great alarm nationwide to the friendly societies, and several – the Manchester Oddfellows, for example – responded by rapidly abolishing their oaths and simplifying their initiations for fear of a backlash against the societies.

Many, if not most, of the fraternal societies of the eighteenth century had had charitable funds for distressed members and for good causes in general, rather than entitlement to benefits as had the friendly societies. But in the early nineteenth century many societies, such as the Oddfellows, that had previously found a voluntary charity fund quite adequate began to feel the need to have stated benefits that members could claim as of right. Government policy on poverty had something to do with this. The Poor Law Amendment Act of 1834 was overtly punitive in intent towards the poor; the idea was to make state charity so unpleasant that the poor would be forced to practise thrift to avoid accepting it. The old practice of 'outdoor relief', by which poor people living in their own homes could receive hand-outs from the parish to help them get by, was abolished; from now on poor relief was given only in grim sex-segregated workhouses. Additional horror was cast over the workhouses by the Anatomy Act of 1822, which gave medical schools the right to dissect the bodies of people who died in workhouses or pauper hospitals – a fate previously reserved for hanged criminals. While the main object of this Act was undoubtedly to further medical research and end the scandal of grave-robbing to supply medical schools, it was widely felt by the poor that by this Act the law was equating poverty with felony. The prospect of ending up not merely in a pauper's grave but on a dissecting slab gave impetus to numerous insurance companies and non-social collecting clubs offering solely burial expenses, but also stimulated membership of the friendly societies proper and encouraged societies that had previously been generally fraternal with a charitable fund to offer regular benefits. It also gave rise to a number of splits within societies, as part of the society opted for full friendly-society status and the rest decided to carry on as a fraternal society with charity funds. Although the 'friendly' factions in such a split did not always register themselves officially, their records are often easier to trace than those of the 'fraternal' groups, which were under no obligation to publish their accounts or register with anyone.

For friendly societies, safeguarding members' funds meant conformity to Friendly Societies Acts. But the government's concept of friendly societies was that they were purely a way for the working classes to save money; from this point of view regalia, rituals and feasts were just a waste. The working classes themselves generally felt that conviviality and sociability were a legitimate and important object of their societies. The registered societies suffered a constant tension between these two ideals, as the government framed regulations to suppress spending on sociability and the societies found ways around the regulations. For example, registered societies were forbidden to spend their funds on beer for meetings; this regulation was traditionally evaded by paying the pub landlord over the odds for hire of the club room, on the unwritten understanding that a full barrel of beer would be in the room. The Registrar for the Friendly Societies was aware that such devices were being used but found it impossible to stamp them out.

Club feasts, which most friendly societies held at least once a year, were another aspect of society activity that their members, if not the government, felt to be vitally important; so much so that even the government regulators gave up trying to prevent societies spending money on them. The officers of the societies unanimously repeated their view that without the feast they could not sustain the members' support: 'They don't see no good in a club without it, they say.' On the feast day, typically the whole society would parade through its town or village with banners, behind a band if it could afford to hire one, all members wearing their regalia and carrying staffs, to a church service and then to the festive meal. In many villages this parade and feast were the highlight of the year. A Wiltshire villager wrote in his memoirs that 'Christmas and Easter were nothing to it; it was, in truth, the red-letter day of all young and old, alike … a great number of folk attended from neighbouring villages; all the old people made it their business to come to 'Maason Club'.' Early in the nineteenth century these festivities could become quite rowdy, with a good deal of drunkenness; as the Victorian period wore on the societies earnestly strove to restrain this aspect of the proceedings, and decorum generally prevailed.

Not everyone shared the societies' enthusiasm for their processions, however. On 29th July 1837 the *Manx Liberal* carried the following hostile report on a Rechabite procession:

TEE-TOTAL AND RECHABITE ANNIVERSARY MEETING.
'All the world's a stage.
And all the men and women merely players.'

The truth of the above lines of our immortal Bard, are every day more and more confirmed, for scarcely has one silly pageant passed from our view [lodges of Oddfellows had recently been formed in the Isle of Man, and the newspaper had taken exception to the extravagance and pomp of their processions already], but another, if possible still sillier, is ready to supply its place, and the rival candidates for absurd distinction, jostle each other on the stage for precedence. We were led into this train of thinking by the motley exhibition of Tuesday last. With the nature of tee-totalism, no one can find fault, we feel favourably disposed towards it, from the great and obvious benefit it has conferred on society, being mainly instrumental in removing from it many vile and revolting scenes of self-debasement and self-sacrifice; – good indeed must be that institution or society, let it be Rechabite Tee-total, Temperance, or what it may, which has the power to arrest the steps of man on the downward path to perdition, and that too at a time when all other stay has lost its power and efficacy. This could all be accomplished, and men, however vile; could return to that line of duty they had so recklessly left, without all this parade of flags, stars, gilt sparrows, inverted wine glasses, scarfs, medals, rosettes and such masonic or odd fellow-looking trumpery, without having recourse to
'The thundering drum,
Or the vile squeaking of the wry-neck'd fife,'
and filling our peaceable old town with all the tumult and noise of a general election.

Societies suffered constant splits throughout the nineteenth century as they decided whether to register and conform to each new Act or do without legal recognition; right until the end of the century there were societies that refused to register. The legislation itself encouraged this tendency. Until 1875 every lodge of an order was required to register and pay the registration fee individually – thus if it had a disagreement with its parent body it was very easy for the lodge to cut its tie and carry on independently, since it already existed in law as a corporate body.

Fear of political sedition and sectarianism continued through the 1830s, with Chartism and agitation for parliamentary reform. The government was still intensely nervous of anything that looked like political activity in lodge-based societies. The Orange Order had been brought from Ireland by military lodges to England, where it seems to have functioned at first very much as a Protestant friendly society. By the 1830s the Orange Order in England had its own English

Below: *Pressed metal figure of William III, Orange Order.*

Above: *Silk collarette of the Orange Order, with a silver jewel.*

Below: *Past master's jewel of an Orange lodge.*

Grand Lodge, with numerous lodges up and down the country, especially in the military. The sectarian nature of Orangeism and its very strong following in the military were felt to have potential for political subversion, possibly even a political coup, and in spite of having a royal prince, the Duke of Cumberland, as its Grand Master the English Orange Order was abolished in 1836.

By the mid nineteenth century fear of revolution and sedition began to fade. Gradually the friendly societies were able to differentiate themselves from trade unions and worked hard at toning down the rowdier aspects of their festivities to achieve respectability. Many friendly societies around this time were actually founded, or heavily supported, by local dignitaries who

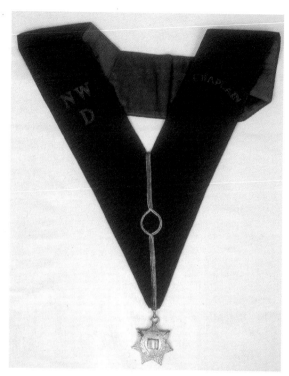

Collar of the Reverend E. L. Wright, Chaplain to the North West Division of the Ancient Order of Druids, early twentieth century.

wanted to help their local poor and keep down the Poor Rate (the local tax for support of the poor, levied on local householders). These societies generally did not entail much conviviality, ceremony or regalia wearing and as a result were generally less popular with the working classes. Gradually the 'affiliated orders' – that is, the multi-lodge societies such as the Oddfellows and the Foresters – gained ground at the expense of single-lodge local or trade-based societies, as they had a sounder actuarial base (small societies could very easily fail), they could help people who needed to travel to seek work – and they had more and better regalia and banners!

Despite the arcane nature of some of the societies' rituals the Church rarely seems to have made any objection to them. It was commonplace for both friendly and fraternal societies to have a chaplain to say grace at the festive board and, just as in medieval times, it was normal for friendly societies' annual festivals to take place on a church holiday (traditionally Whitsun) and to include a procession to church for a special service with a sermon. The practice of attending members' funerals with regalia and banners, and sometimes of holding a society ceremony at the graveside in addition to the church burial service, seems to have been acceptable to the majority of the clergy; only occasional instances are recorded of clergymen objecting to this activity. However, objections were sometimes made: in 1835 the Vicar of Leeds refused an invitation to preach a sermon at the Leeds Oddfellows' annual procession on the grounds that he did 'not preach sermons for Oddfellows, or anything of that kind'; and in 1841 the Archdeacon of Durham instructed the clergy of his diocese not to allow the Oddfellows' practice of 'offering public prayers and

Tie-pin and lapel pin of the New Zealand Druids.

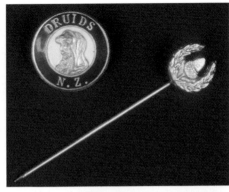

making orations at the graves of their comrades', describing this custom as 'contempt of our holy office, and the desecration of our holy places', and advised clergymen to appeal to the ecclesiastical courts if their refusal to permit these ceremonies were 'overborne by force or clamour'.

The fraternal and friendly societies spread throughout the Americas and the British Empire; they were perhaps even more useful in developing countries, where they provided emigrants and newly created townships with ready-made social networks. An interesting feature in the light of this is that the British societies were generally multi-racial – almost the only multi-racial social groupings in the Empire. This in many cases formed a point of friction between the British societies and their American offshoots; in 1889 the Ancient Order of Foresters preferred to let the American

Jewel of a past Chief Ranger of the Canadian Foresters – note the maple leaf and beaver.

Jewel of a past Chief Ranger of the Canadian Foresters – note the Canadian moose rather than the British Foresters' stag.

Above: *Hat of the American Independent Order of Foresters, made in Chicago c.1880–90. Of contemporary naval style.*

Left: *Presentation jewel of the Loyal United Lodge of the Sons of Israel to their Honorary Secretary, Samuel Lawton, 1836.*

Collar of the Order of Ancient Maccabeans, of velvet with gold and silver embroidery and a gold fringe.

20

Foresters break away completely rather than approve its operating of a colour bar.

The American lodge-based societies, which had not had to contend with hostile legislation, generally went in for even more elaborate and colourful ritual and regalia; in many of them the members routinely wore not only regalia but entire costumes for their meetings and processions. After the end of the American Civil War there was a fashion for using surplus army uniforms as a basis for the costume, which gave the societies a semi-military appearance.

In the colonies and in the United States the friendly-society movement spread to non-English-speaking communities, and returning emigrants from those communities took the societies back to their countries of origin. The United Ancient Order of Druids in particular acquired a significant following in Germany and Scandinavia. Within Britain many immigrant groups adopted the friendly-society model as a basis for mutual help in their communities and very often adopted the conventions of friendly-society regalia as well. One such group was the Order of Ancient Maccabeans Friendly Society, which lasted at least from 1911 to 1978.

Women had participated in the friendly-society movement from the beginning, on separate though similar lines to the men. (It seems to have been universally taken for granted that the sexes should not mix in fraternal societies; in this they differed markedly from the medieval guilds. The first society to have mixed-sex membership within its lodges was the American Independent Order of Good Templars, founded in 1851, and it remained unique in this respect for decades.) Already in the eighteenth century there were large numbers of women's societies; in 1794 about 15 per cent of the 542 registered societies in London were for women. The women seem to have valued the social aspect as much as the men did; their rules typically provided for this by insisting on regular attendance, banning the presence of husbands and children, who might have disrupted the proceedings, and (up to the mid nineteenth century, when tea began to appear) specifying the provision of beer. Thus the societies provided a unique space for exclusively female social interaction.

Sash of a female member of the temperance Order of the Phoenix, possibly a Past Chief Matron.

21

Even more remarkably, women's societies normally had an annual public procession wearing regalia, followed by a feast, just as the men had. In 1833 the Markfield Female Friendly Society in Leicestershire, founded in 1823, laid down the rules for its Whit Monday feast:

> every member who is not above five miles from the club-house shall attend by eleven o'clock in the morning (unless prevented by illness) or forfeit 1d. Every member shall attend the minister to and from the church appearing in a decent orderly dress and behaviour, each having a staff at their own expense; and every member that doth not obey and walk two and two and obey orders shall forfeit 2 pence.

The Markfield women's society, just like male societies, required members to attend at fellow members' funerals, for which each member was expected to provide 'a white ribband and a pair of white gloves'. It was also specified that 'any member being disguised in liquor at the time shall forfeit 6d'. The society was dissolved in 1925, after having provided financial support and a same-sex social network to the women of Markfield for just over a century.

In the eighteenth and nineteenth centuries the friendly societies created almost the only type of public occasion in which women featured in their own right rather than accompanying their menfolk. They were not shy about it either; often they would hire a band for their annual procession. This did shock many respectable members of society. The *Manx Liberal*, which greatly disapproved of friendly-society processions, expressed in its report a particular shock at women's marching in a public procession at all:

> but even admitting the utility of the procession, as regards the males, we know not a more ridiculous, nay, revolting spectacle than that of the rosy cheeked daughters of our Isle — against whom it would be foul and wrong even to breathe a suspicion injurious to their virtues — to see them parading our streets and forming a conspicuous part in the procession, and courting observation, — the retiring from which is women's greatest charm, and allowing the world to judge that their practices must have been the most abandoned, to justify each a humiliation, in which

> 'They roughen to the sense,
> And all the winning softness of the sex is lost.'

The women's societies, which had always been poorer than the men's because of lower female incomes, came under pressure in the later nineteenth century from this Victorian notion that women, even those of the working classes, should stay in the home. Women's employment was increasingly restricted to the poorest sectors of society, and many women's societies folded. Temperance friendly societies had almost from their beginnings enrolled women, though generally in separate lodges. Gradually, towards the end of the century, the affiliated orders began to admit women, initially also in separate lodges.

Juvenile lodges began to emerge in the mid nineteenth century. They too suffered difficulties with the law; it took several revisions of the legislation before their status was settled satisfactorily in 1895. The main direct benefit parents got from enrolling their children in friendly societies was payment of their medical expenses, or, in the worst case, funeral expenses; but the juvenile lodges also functioned as youth clubs and would organise sports and educational activities for their members. Temperance societies in particular valued their juvenile branches as a means of influencing young minds against alcohol and put much effort into promoting them and making them attractive to the young.

Obverse (left) and reverse of a jewel of the United Juvenile Order of the Total Abstinent Sons of the Phoenix, presented to Dora Dudley 'for past services' in 1929. Dora would have been about eleven years old at the time, and it seems she had already held a senior post in her lodge.

By the second half of the century the 'affiliated orders' had succeeded in shedding suspicion of political subversion or rowdiness and had become respectable. At the Great Exhibition of 1851 there were days specially reserved for friendly societies to visit, and observers were impressed by their decorous and orderly behaviour. The Foresters indeed made an annual outing to Crystal Palace from 1869 onwards.

The societies were by now a familiar feature in civic life; mayors and other dignitaries attended friendly-society occasions and the societies participated in and added colour to public events. Their social activities could be on a quite startlingly lavish scale; the *Foresters' Miscellany and Quarterly Review* of October 1862 reported a number of local jamborees such as this one:

> Tovil, Kent – The members of Court *Victory*, 3477, celebrated their second anniversary on Monday the 28th July. The brethren met in the High-street, Maidstone, and, headed by the band of the Cavalry Depot, marched in procession to Tovil. The village being most gaily decorated with flags and streamers, presented a very pleasing appearance; more especially the mansion and beautiful grounds of Mrs Makinnon, who had kindly granted the use of her park and grounds for the day. Dinner was provided by Br. Smith, in a large marquee in the park. ... After the removal of the cloth, the usual loyal and patriotic toasts were drunk ... the band playing appropriate music between each

Obverse and reverse of a medal commemorating an Ancient Order of Foresters visit to Crystal Palace.

Cover of the 'Foresters' Miscellany and Quarterly Review', October 1862.

toast. The Secretary read the report of the Society for the past year... The Coxheath Juvenile Drum and Fife Band then marched on the ground and played a selection of popular airs, and continued playing at intervals during the afternoon. A quadrille band provided amusement for those fond of a dance, while archery and cricket found numerous patrons. Tea was provided in a tent at the foot of a grassy slope; and the old folks enjoyed the balmy breezes under the shade of the wide-spreading elms, while the young folks were playing at kiss-in-the-ring to their hearts' content. The last, but not least, interesting event of the day, was the ascent of a magnificent balloon, made by Br. Waller, its height being 17½ feet, with letters around it in coloured paper one foot in length –

Jewel of a Past Prince Rat of the Water Rats.

ancient order of foresters. As it arose majestically in the air, several rounds of applause were given by the thousands present. The weather proved all that could be desired. It is supposed that no fewer than between 6,000 and 7,000 persons visited the park during the day. Nothing occurred to mar the enjoyments.

By the turn of the century an immense proportion of the male population of Britain, and a fair number of the female, belonged to a regalia-wearing body. The friendly societies had an enormous membership – it has been estimated that there may have been as many as nine and a half million friendly-society members in Britain in 1910. In addition there were all the fraternal groups: the Freemasons, the Buffaloes, and others. Fraternity and its regalia were such an accepted feature of British life that quite unrelated groups found it natural to adopt its conventions. The theatrical fraternity of the Water Rats, founded to do charitable work for children and retired actors, gave each other titles such as Prince Rat and Lady Rat and wore jewels quite consistent with the fraternal tradition. The Conservative support group, the Primrose League, gave its members badges denoting their status in the hierarchy in the same way. Even

Group of jewels of the Primrose League.

'Jewels' of two degrees of the Ancient Order of Frothblowers.

wholly frivolous groups adopted the 'fraternal order' model in order to carry on their activities, just as eighteenth-century clubs had done; a case in point is the Ancient Order of Frothblowers, a beer-drinking club with charitable purpose that flourished between the world wars and awarded rank and regalia for making recruits to the order.

But social changes brought difficulties. Friendly-society benefits had never normally included old-age pensions, but with increasing life expectancy many societies found themselves with numbers of elderly members on long-term

sickness benefit, which had financially much the same effect as paying out pensions. This made their finances untenable, and gradually it became clear that state provision was ultimately the only solution.

Most of the major orders, still distrustful of state interference, were ambivalent about the introduction of state old-age pensions; they argued that if anyone could receive them, irrespective of their moral character and of whether they had made any attempt to provide for themselves, this would place 'a premium on improvidence and a discount on thrift'. However, the introduction in 1908 of old-age pensions (for the over seventies) took considerable financial strain off the societies.

Lloyd George's National Insurance Act of 1911 brought in contributory unemployment and sickness benefit. All wage earners had to enrol in authorised institutions through which their contributions were paid; these institutions included friendly societies, insurance

Jewel of the National Conference of Friendly Societies – the forerunner of the present-day Association of Friendly Societies.

26

companies, burial clubs and trade unions. Convivial friendly societies opened special sections for members who wanted only the National Insurance without the social activity.

The National Insurance Act greatly increased the membership of many of the larger friendly societies, but these increased numbers came at a cost. By accepting the special sections the societies had finally given in to the long-held government attitude that the real business of the friendly societies was financial provision and that sociability and conviviality were optional extras. Moreover, in order to become approved institutions, the societies were required to open the main society, not just the special sections, to all applicants and abolish obstacles to membership such as oaths and signs.

Now that the friendly societies had a whole group of members who did not participate in the rituals and sociability that members in earlier times had set such store by and often risked criminal prosecution to maintain, during the years between the world wars these customs gradually started to fall into disuse. This trend was accelerated by changes in social life and particularly in patterns of leisure; with radio, cinema and the increasing availability of motor transport, competing kinds of leisure activity became popular. In even the remotest villages the monthly society meeting and the annual procession and feast were no longer the only entertainments available.

The Second World War formed a watershed in many aspects of British social life, and the social activities of the friendly and fraternal societies, their meetings, processions and feasts, shared in the general social disruption caused by the war. Once the habit and tradition of public processions and festivities had been broken, in the post-war era many of them were never revived; they were felt to belong the past. In the youth culture of the later twentieth century the social atmosphere of the fraternal societies – single-sex, formal, suit-and-tie occasions – found less and less favour with the young. Membership gradually fell, and several of the fraternal societies, such as the Ancient Order of Druids, eventually died out.

The decline of the benefit societies was steeper; the implementation of the 'Bevin reforms' after the Second World War was disastrous for them. National Insurance was now to be administered directly by the state rather than through the approved institutions, and the free National Health Service did away with the need for medical benefits altogether. In the second half of the twentieth century the benefit societies shrank in membership, amalgamated, re-amalgamated, and many were finally wound up altogether. However, a small nucleus of friendly societies hung on, many keeping themselves in business by specialising in savings policies appropriate to people on low incomes, for whom the high-street banks and

An example of the modest insignia worn by friendly-society officers in the second half of the twentieth century and, in some cases, still worn today.

the big pensions companies had nothing appropriate to offer. Some are purely mutual financial institutions but more of them than one might expect still wear at least some regalia, and some (such as the Oddfellows and the Foresters) still maintain social activities for those members who want them.

By the end of the twentieth century, however, the surviving friendly-society movement saw signs that the wheel might be turning once more. Governments began to hint that the state could no longer aspire to provide adequate pensions and advised citizens to make provision for their old age. The National Health Service began to look inadequate to the demands made on it; health insurance increasingly looked like prudence rather than a luxury. Scandals in the big banks and pensions companies gave rise to widespread disillusionment and distrust of financial services providers. It is possible that the mutually owned sociable society may yet find a new lease of life in the twenty-first century.

Friendly society artefacts

Most friendly- and fraternal-society material displays a striking family resemblance. This resemblance is often vaguely ascribed to 'Masonic influence' – and certainly the Freemasons were very influential – but it does seem generally true that all the various groups were drawing on a common folk tradition of civic and guild dress and custom, which prescribed a similar range of artefacts, mostly heavily symbolic in nature.

The artefacts of these societies comprise one of the richest areas of British folk art. Early items were often made by hand, and each lodge might have a different design or style. Symbolism from a wide variety of sources was used and given new meanings by the members themselves.

There was a general development from hand-made, and often home-made, items in earlier centuries to machine-made articles produced by big specialised businesses (and sold by the societies themselves, who reckoned to make a profit from the sale of approved regalia to members). Three of the largest manufacturers, whose trade names appear constantly on regalia, were Henry Slingsby, George Kenning and George Tutill. Henry Slingsby of Nuneaton specialised in high-quality jacquard weaving, enabling silk collars and sashes to be decorated with elaborate emblems and lettering at relatively low cost. George Kenning (now trading as Toye Kenning & Spencer Limited, still specialist Masonic suppliers) produced printed silk panels to be stitched to the front of aprons or the breast of sashes, and George Tutill supplied friendly societies and trade unions alike with a wide range of banners, regalia and jewels. Tutill's speciality was in producing standardised shapes and designs,

Right: *Jacquard-woven silk sash of the Ancient Order of Foresters, pre-1892. Jacquard weaving made elaborate decoration possible at a cheap price for the large societies.*

Below: *Jewel of the Loyal Order of Ancient Shepherds (Ashton Unity), in pressed brass, typical of the cheap regalia mass-produced by George Tutill.*

Six early-nineteenth-century Oddfellows' aprons, hand-painted on lambskin. Each is an individual work of folk art.

Home-embroidered apron of the Ancient Order of Foresters. The Foresters had mass-produced regalia from the middle of the nineteenth century, so whoever owned this apron either could not afford the official regalia or preferred to make his or her own.

which could be produced at a relatively low cost – at the price of making one's society look remarkably like dozens of others equipped by Tutill.

However, the trend from hand-made to factory-made was by no means a steady progression; ready-printed Masonic aprons were already being marketed in the eighteenth century, whereas home-made banners and aprons were still being painted or embroidered by members of smaller or poorer societies into the twentieth.

REGALIA

Perhaps the most commonly occurring pieces are the items that society members wore for society rituals: these are known collectively as 'regalia'. Ultimately the idea of wearing regalia derived from the guild tradition; the officers of medieval guilds had typically worn chains of office, special robes and so on, as civic dignitaries and officers of London livery companies still do. The idea of the craftsman's apron was added to this. The neck-chain, shoulder-sash and breast star of orders of chivalry also had an influence; jewels of fraternal societies in the Georgian and Regency periods were often based on the star of the Garter or the Bath. In early societies items were made individually, sometimes home-made, and thus lodges and individuals had a good deal of leeway in the exact form of the regalia. As the large orders became more organised in the nineteenth century they increasingly had standardised regalia made by nominated suppliers; for many of the friendly societies the sale of approved regalia was a significant source of income.

Apron

The apron is perhaps the most characteristic item of regalia, and the one that typifies fraternal societies, and particularly Freemasonry, in the public mind. It

Jewel box of the Ancient Order of Foresters. Sale of regalia was profitable for the large affiliated orders.

Full set of regalia worn by a member of the Roll of Honour degree of the Royal Antediluvian Order of Buffaloes. Although the style of these items is specific to the RAOB, a similar set of items – apron, collar, sash and gauntlets – was worn by many different societies.

Apron of the Ancient Order of Free Gardeners: blue cloth with a velvet flap, gold fringe and applied gold braid. The Free Gardeners, of Scottish origin, have a semicircular flap like that of the Scottish Masons.

has its origin in the protective apron worn by working men in the seventeenth and eighteenth centuries. This apron was fastened by ties taken around the waist and tied in front, and had a bib that was usually attached to a waistcoat button. Workmen in different trades used aprons of different materials, shapes and colours, and in some trades there was a distinction between the aprons of skilled workers and their juniors – so even before the societies adopted them they were a well-understood badge of membership of a group and sometimes of hierarchy within that group.

It became traditional in the fraternal societies to unfasten the apron from the waistcoat button and let the bib hang down in a flap over the front; this flap often became stylised into a decorative feature. In English Masonry it was eventually standardised to a triangular shape, with two decorative hanging tags representing the ends of the waist-ties; the

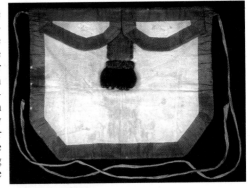

Two double-curved Oddfellows' aprons. The tassels hanging from the flaps are relics of the waist-ties that used to be fastened in front.

Apron of the Manchester Unity of Oddfellows. A printed silk panel is bound with silk ribbon, overlaid with gold fringe and two different patterns of openwork gold lace, and there is a rosette of silver spangles and glass jewels in each lower corner.

Buffalo apron is very similar. Scottish Masonic aprons by contrast had a semicircular flap. Characteristic of many Oddfellow aprons is a double-semicircle flap, though others have a single-semicircle flap or none at all.

There was any number of different ways to ornament the apron. White lambskin aprons offered an ideal surface for painting or printing, and early examples are often beautiful specimens of folk art. Silk aprons could also be painted, though increasingly throughout the nineteenth century commercially printed silk squares were used. The edges could be bound with gold lace or silk ribbon and ornamented with gold fringe. Embroidery of all kinds was used, from home-made silk or wool work to professional gold work similar to that used on church or state robes. Extra decorative elements could be applied, for example gold or silk tassels, rosettes, pompoms or pressed metal plaques.

The symbolic apron tended to be smaller than the full-size protective apron of the workman, but not always; some societies (some branches of the Free Gardeners, for instance) wore ankle-length aprons without flaps. Where the waist-ties of such aprons do not survive it is often hard to tell them from small banners.

Collar

The collar derives from the collars worn in orders of chivalry and as badges of office in civic life by guild officers, lord mayors and the like. In many societies the collar also signified the holding of some office, either past or present, or some special distinction, and was not worn by all members.

The form of the collar varied greatly. Some are very like mayoral chains, being made of decorated metal links, often supported on a textile backing, with a pendant ornament at the centre front. (When the collar is that of a lodge officer, this pendant is usually symbolic of the office held.) Some are made of straight widths of silk, mitred to fit over the shoulders, and come down to a point at the centre front, usually with a pendant or applied jewel. Others might be shaped in a variety of ways, some almost resembling small capes. Shaped textile collars frequently had embroidered or applied decoration or lettering at breast level.

Above: *Chain collar of the Manchester Unity of Oddfellows, decorative but cheaply made in pressed metal.*

Oddfellows' collar, of silk with a central breast jewel in gold and enamel.

Collarette of the Nottingham Imperial Order of Oddfellows – a simple silk ribbon with a small jewel.

Collarette

The collarette, also sometimes called a neck-ribbon, could also be a badge of office but, unlike the collar, in some societies it was worn by all members. It might also be used to denote members of a higher or 'side' order within the group. It was usually a simple straight ribbon strip of silk, sometimes mitred over the shoulders, terminating in front either with a pendant jewel or a tassel. One common type was made of jacquard-woven silk, in which the society's emblem and the status of the owner – 'Honorary Member', 'Secretary', 'Past Chief Ranger' – could be depicted. Thus a similar item of regalia could be used to denote the different roles of members.

The collarette, being inexpensive and not too eccentric looking, is still worn by some friendly societies who have abandoned the more elaborate and exotic elements of their old regalia – the Ancient Order of Foresters, for example.

Gauntlets

Gauntlets were originally gauntlet gloves; gradually the cuff part of the gloves became more elaborately decorated and was often made of non-launderable materials such as velvet and gold lace. The expense of replacing

Gauntlets of a Knight of the Golden Horn, in velvet with gold embroidery. Very similar gauntlets are worn in the Buffaloes and used to be widely worn in Freemasonry. Today they are worn by the Master and lodge officers in only a few Masonic lodges.

Sash of the Order of Rechabites, in silk ribbon with applied pressed-metal jewel and gold bullions.

such gloves when they got dirty was too great, so it became customary for the decorative cuffs of the gloves to be made as separate items so that the gloves proper could be washed or replaced as necessary.

Sash

The sash was one of the commonest symbols of society membership. Early societies often referred to it as a 'ribbon' (this is still the technical term for the sash of orders of chivalry such as the Garter and the Bath), and often it really was just a long piece of broad ribbon; more elaborate versions were of silk or velvet on a backing. It was worn over the shoulder and fastened at the hip, either with silk or Russia-braid ties or, from the second half of the nineteenth century, by one of a variety of patent fastenings.

Sashes of poorer societies might have home-made embroidery or stencilled lettering. Jacquard-woven decoration was also relatively inexpensive, as were pressed-metal ornaments and silk panels printed with the order's emblem. Those of more affluent groups might have gold embroidery and gold or silver bullion fringe at the ends and sometimes on the shoulder.

Below left: Velvet sash of a Past Chief Noble (PCN) of the Phoenix, embroidered in silver.
Below right: Jacquard-woven sash of the Ancient Order of Foresters, post-1892.

Portrait photograph of a member of the Ancient Order of Foresters, c.1910.

Jewels

These items are called 'jewels' by the societies and by their manufacturers, although they need not be elaborate or made of precious materials. (In the eighteenth century the badges of orders of chivalry were referred to as 'jewels'; fraternal and friendly societies retain this usage.) Breast jewels were worn pinned to the jacket, like military medals, or sometimes to the sash, if one was worn; neck jewels were worn on a collarette or neck-ribbon. Photographs of friendly-society members often show an impressive collection of jewels, since there were a variety of reasons for which breast jewels were presented.

Above left: Secretary's jewel of the Manchester Unity of Oddfellows.

Above right: Jewel of a Past Chief Noble of the United Grand Order of the Total Abstinent Sons of the Phoenix, with symbols including Death and Mercury in the central roundel, 1889.

Members' jewels: in some societies every member wore a jewel, most often a breast jewel, with the symbol of the society.

Officers' jewels: these were worn in most societies. Each officer would wear a jewel with the symbol of his office, usually on a collar or collarette. It was rare for these to be privately owned; generally the lodge would have a set and they would be handed on to the new appointee at the end of a term of office. Therefore, although officers' jewels were widely used, they are relatively rare, and they generally have no name inscribed on them.

Past officers' jewels: in lodges that could afford it, when a member completed his term of office as Treasurer, Noble Arch Druid, or whatever other role it might be, the lodge would raise the money to present him with a jewel. These are usually inscribed on the reverse (much more rarely on the obverse) with the date and the name of the recipient and the lodge. A typical inscription might be: 'Presented to Bro. John Smith by the Brothers of Jubilee Lodge No 322 as a mark of respect for past services, 13th June 1905'. Sometimes the inscription helpfully gives the name of the society and specifies what office Brother John Smith had fulfilled (for example, 'his services as Secretary') – but more often not!

Founder's jewel, Manchester Unity of Oddfellows.

Charity jewels: friendly and fraternal societies alike raised money for charities as well as for benefits to their own members. Fraternal societies – in particular the Freemasons and Buffaloes – encouraged this by presenting medals to members who had given or raised large sums.

Founders' jewels: lodges were typically founded by a quorum of members from established lodges meeting to create the new one. Each of the members taking part might then be presented with a founder's jewel.

Commemorative jewels: all sorts of occasions might be marked by the issue of a commemorative jewel – a conference, a congress, a centenary celebration or even a royal jubilee or wedding wholly unrelated to the organisation itself. Many societies held an annual moveable conference (AMC) – the friendly-society equivalent of an annual general meeting – and might issue commemorative jewels to the delegates.

Other items of costume also occasionally figured: in the Ancient Order of Druids beards and white robes were worn, the Guardians of the Ashton Unity Shepherds had big coats and broad-brimmed hats, and in photographs of society processions it is quite common to see the officers and banner-bearers in some special kind of robe or coat. But such costumes were always much rarer than jewels and regalia, and do not often survive.

Honorary members' regalia

Many societies had a rule that no 'gentleman' could become a member. However, they often needed the services of professional people – a doctor, a solicitor, an accountant – and the normal solution was to make them honorary members. Also, many societies set up under the patronage of upper-class people gave their patrons honorary membership. Honorary members would often have distinctively marked regalia, and this is quite commonly found.

Royal Antediluvian Order of Buffaloes commemorative jewel of the Silver Jubilee of Queen Elizabeth II.

Mourning apron of the Ancient Order of Foresters – the printed panel has a deathbed and a graveside scene.

Mourning regalia

As well as being able to pay for a decent funeral, people in the eighteenth and nineteenth centuries generally felt it important to have it well attended. Friendly and fraternal societies aimed to meet this need also; they typically had a rule obliging the brethren or sisters to attend the funeral of a fellow member of their lodge, dressed in mourning. Sometimes this just meant black armbands and hatbands as was normal at the time, but very often special mourning regalia were worn. This might simply be the usual costume with the addition of some black rosettes, but many lodges kept complete sets of special mourning regalia, with all the textile parts black or black-edged. In 1815 the Manchester

Mourning apron of the Grand Lodge of Kent Independent Order of Oddfellows, in lambskin with black ribbon.

Two Oddfellows' mourning aprons in printed white silk with black trimming.

Oddfellows specified that the 'death supporters' should carry drawn swords in the procession. Some lodges could even afford to buy their officers black coats for funerals. Dressed in this way, the lodge members would walk two by two in the funeral procession. Many societies, such as the Oddfellows and the Foresters, had standard funeral orations, which would be delivered at the deceased member's house, or at the graveside, or both. Friendly societies believed that the sight of these impressive ceremonies encouraged many people to join them.

OTHER KINDS OF ARTEFACTS

Equipment for meetings: lodges that could afford it would equip their lodge room with suitable furniture, such as ceremonial chairs for their officers, wall boards listing the names of past officers, and so on. Very often the guards

Manchester Unity of Oddfellows loving-cup.

Right: *Free Gardeners' brass vesta box.*

whose duty it was to keep strangers out of the meeting would be equipped with ceremonial weaponry – swords or axes for example. The lodge master might have a mace, sceptre or gavel. The manufacture of items for use by lodges and chapters was often very carefully thought through. Druid lodge chairs could be massive, decorated with the 'Tau Delta' symbol and oak leaves in imitation of medieval styles. Sometimes the very fabric of the items was symbolic; one Masonic lodge was presented with chairs made from the wood of old Putney Bridge by a lodge of that name to 'bridge the gap' between them. Even items such as powder horns, shepherds' crooks and drinking vessels exist with crudely drawn or engraved emblems.

Equipment for social activity: the social refreshments that followed the formal meeting would require utensils such as beer mugs, jugs, glasses, punch-bowls, loving-cups, tobacco pipes, snuffboxes and – particularly in the case of temperance groups – teapots and teacups. All of these might be specially made for the society and decorated with its emblem. The materials used range from silver and fine Chinese porcelain to cheap popular English ceramics such as Sunderland lustreware.

Objects for the home and for personal use: home decoration in the eighteenth and nineteenth centuries frequently displayed signs of membership. Longcase clocks exist with Masonic and Oddfellow faces; certificates of membership were designed to be framed and set on the wall. The most modest everyday items such as match cases, trivets for flat-irons, bed warming-pans and even jelly moulds could be enhanced by fraternal images. In day-to-day life Victorian men's dress presented few opportunities for such display, but the symbols of one's society could be carried on watch fobs and seals, spectacle cases, tie-pins and lapel badges, and some of the Masonic orders adopted rings with reversible

Longcase clock with Oddfellows' symbols.

Above: *Loyal Ancient Order of Shepherds flat-iron stand.*
Left: *Masonic flat-iron stand.*

44

Above: *Lapel pin of Ye Olde Friends.*

Right: *Lapel pin of the Ancient Order of Foresters.*

Two lapel pins of the Free Gardeners.

centres. In the same way many fraternal ceramics were decorated differently on each side, so that on a mantelpiece a non-fraternal side could be displayed when membership was not to be declared. The use of this type of distinctive imagery gradually diminished in the years leading up to the Second World War.

Gifts: lodges of male-only societies often held 'ladies' nights' for the wives of members, at which a gift would be presented to each lady guest. Very often these were inscribed with the name of the lodge and the occasion of their presentation.

Books and other printed matter: all societies needed rule books, ritual books and minute books; many also had songbooks, as group singing was a popular feature of society sociability. Most of the larger societies produced a periodical, such as the *Foresters' Miscellany* and the *Oddfellows' Magazine.* It was important for members who moved to another part of the country to be able to prove their membership to the lodge in their new neighbourhood, so printed membership certificates were given to new initiates; these were often elaborately decorated, and were intended to be framed and displayed. Other printed ephemera such as invitations, programmes and tickets to events were also produced and sometimes survive.

Photographs: studio portraits of society members in full regalia frequently turn up in attics and 'bygones' shops; pictures of public events such as

Oddfellows' song sheet.

Portrait of a senior Druid.

Annual report of the Manchester Unity of Oddfellows.

*'The Complete Manual of Oddfellowship',
1873.*

processions and Masonic foundation-stone layings turn up rather more rarely, although these are often to be found in newspaper archives.

Objects for public processions: all societies made a point of looking their best at their public outings; in impoverished lodges the ceremonial sashes might be stored carefully in a box all year round and issued only for the annual procession and feast. Banners would be carried, either home-made or made by a specialist banner-painting firm such as George Tutill, often with decorative pole finials, and the members carried staves, which might also have finials.

*Membership
certificate of the
Ancient Order of
Druids.*

The sign of the Freemasons' Arms pub in Long Acre, London WC2.

REMAINS IN THE LANDSCAPE

Until the early nineteenth century societies mostly met in public houses. In villages there was often nowhere else where a room could be hired; but even in towns an inn or tavern was generally the venue of choice, and even gentlemen found it quite normal to hold their meetings there. Many pubs relied on the monthly rent and beer sales from lodge meetings and became so associated with the society that met there that they took their name from it. The origins of some such names, including the Freemasons' Arms and the Oddfellows' Arms, are obvious; others, such as the Foresters' Arms or the Jolly Gardeners, are less so.

The Ancient Foresters pub in Galleywall Road, Bermondsey, London SE16.

An example of a street named 'Freemasons Road'. This one is in Canning Town, London, E16.

As the nineteenth century wore on, drinking in pubs became less respectable, particularly for women. (When the affiliated orders began to admit women they often felt it necessary to rule that no female lodges should meet in licensed premises, and female societies that had originally had beer as the refreshment at their meetings began to change to tea.) By the 1860s alternative venues for meetings existed in most neighbourhoods: schoolrooms, temperance hotels, church halls, mechanics' institutes, working men's clubs. After 1855 it was legally possible for registered friendly societies to own premises, and from then on Oddfellows and Foresters in particular bought or built their own halls, as did the Freemasons. Masonic halls still exist very widely; friendly society halls are now rare, although the buildings often survive. Whole streets might be named after these halls or pubs; there is a sprinkling of names such as 'Oddfellows Place' or 'Freemasons Road' in many English towns, and many streets with 'Gardeners', 'Foresters' or 'Shepherds' in their name may contain a friendly-society connection now discoverable only by local historians.

Symbolism used on the artefacts of friendly and fraternal societies

The friendly and fraternal societies developed at a time when a rich tradition of visual symbols was generally understood and used by society at large; they drew on, elaborated and often altered the meaning of these symbols to suit their own purposes. The origin of such symbols is remarkably varied – classical mythology, the Bible, medieval alchemical ideas, artisan skills and Renaissance humanism all contributed.

Masonic symbolism influenced the other societies greatly; symbols of Masonic origin were used at least occasionally by a wide variety of orders and by some societies. However, it would be unwise to presume that symbols of Masonic origin were used by other societies with the same meaning that the Masons gave them; the societies were all prepared to use these symbols in their own way.

Past officer's jewel of the Bromley Lodge of the Ancient Order of Druids. The prancing horse pinned to the ribbon is the badge of the county of Kent, in which Bromley is – it has no Druidical significance.

SYMBOLS OF LODGE OFFICE

Many jewels were worn specifically to identify the holders of particular offices in their lodges. The set described here are all Masonic, as are the titles attached to them, but very similar badges were used in many societies to identify people fulfilling these roles – though different societies may have called them by different names.

Almoner's purse – Almoner. This is a stylised medieval purse; the heart on the flap indicates that the money within is to be used for charitable purposes.
Quill pen, crossed quills – Secretary. The quill pen symbolises writing and therefore the job of the secretary.

Open book – Chaplain. Generally signifies a sacred book. Usually there is no legible writing on the book; this is deliberate, to allow it to represent any sacred book, rather than specifically the Christian Bible, and therefore not offend or exclude non-Christian members. In Masonry it is referred to for this reason as 'the Volume of the Sacred Law'. But some societies (for example the Nottingham Oddfellows) use it simply as a symbol of knowledge.

Lyre or harp – Organist. The Greek lyre has been a symbol of music in general from classical times. Sometimes the harp, its modern equivalent, is used instead. Music played an important part in the meetings of many societies, from hymns and solemn music to heighten the atmosphere of ritual to convivial singsongs. Few lodges of any society can have had a real organ and organist; a piano, harmonium or something of the kind must always have been more usual. The Ancient Order of Druids had a 'Minstrel'; the Grand Independent Lodge of Ancient Druids in 1823 had the office of 'Grand Pianiste'.

Crossed wands – Director of Ceremonies. A long white wand has been the badge of office of a steward (in the sense of the chief officer of a household) from medieval times. It would have been the responsibility of the medieval steward to cater for the household and marshal formal events. In Masonry these are separate roles; the Steward has the task of catering, and the person with the job of regulating processions and dinners is called Director of Ceremonies.

Cornucopia – Steward. The cornucopia, or horn of plenty, is a symbol of abundance and refers to the catering aspect of the Steward's role.

Key – Treasurer. As in any organisation, the most important function of the Treasurer is keeping the money safe; the symbol of this office is therefore a key or pair of crossed keys.

Sword, Crossed swords – Tyler, Inner Guard. Virtually all lodge-based societies felt that ensuring privacy for their lodge meetings was important, and many required the lodge room to be guarded to prevent non-members entering or overhearing; this was generally done by two guards, one outside the room and one inside. These officers are called Guardian and Outer Guardian in the Ancient Order of Druids, Senior and Junior Beadle in the Ancient Order of Foresters, and so on. The Tyler of a Masonic lodge really does carry a sword; Beadles of Forester courts had ceremonial axes.

THE VIRTUES

In the European tradition there are seven virtues, divided into two sets:

Faith, Hope and Charity: the 'theological virtues', defined by St Paul in his First Epistle to the Corinthians.

Justice, Prudence, Temperance and Fortitude: the 'cardinal virtues', derived from Renaissance and ultimately classical tradition.

Almost all of the friendly and fraternal societies claimed that promoting virtue in their members was one of their aims, so naturally one or the other set of virtues (rarely all seven) often appears on jewels, certificates and regalia. Occasionally Charity is shown on her own; the others normally appear only as part of the set of three or four.

Justice, Prudence, Temperance and Fortitude are depicted as maidens in characteristic poses with their identifying attributes; their iconography goes back to the Middle Ages. Occasionally their attributes alone are shown, but this is rare.

Justice. She holds scales (to weigh guilt and innocence) and a sword (to punish the guilty) and wears a blindfold (to show that she acts impartially).

Prudence. She holds a mirror, symbolising self-knowledge, and may also be accompanied by a serpent, the symbol of wisdom.

Temperance. She holds two jugs and pours liquid from one into the other. This signifies that she is watering her wine. (The virtue of temperance traditionally meant reasonable moderation in general; only in the nineteenth century did it come to mean moderation specifically in drinking alcohol.)

Fortitude. She either thrusts her hand into a fire or, much more rarely, tames a lion.

Faith, Hope and Charity are represented either by maidens holding their symbolic attributes or by these attributes alone.

Faith. Since this set of symbols is a specifically Christian one, Faith's symbol is usually a cross, although very occasionally she carries a book.

Hope. An anchor. This refers to chapter 6 verse 19 of St Paul's Epistle to the Hebrews, 'Hope we have as an anchor of the soul'.

Charity. A heart. This refers to the original meaning of the word 'charity', which is 'brotherly love' rather than just giving to the poor.

But Charity is sometimes shown in a quite different way, depicted either by a scene of a woman caring for little children or by the story of the Good Samaritan; this is perhaps because the heart also symbolises romantic love and could therefore have been misread.

Sometimes the virtues are shown cryptically as a ladder with three, four or seven rungs, the idea being that virtues are the rungs of the ladder by which one reaches heaven. This ladder is sometimes further identified as 'Jacob's ladder', which in the Old Testament led to heaven.

Biblical and moral scenes and symbols frequently appear:

Adam and Eve in the Garden of Eden, with or without the serpent.
Primal innocence and the fall of man.

A little child with lion and lamb (the Peaceable Kingdom in Isaiah, chapter 11 verses 1–10).
The ultimate triumph of good and godliness.

Noah's Ark, with or without the rainbow and the dove with olive branch; sometimes the rainbow or the dove appears alone, as occasionally does the olive branch.
The story of Noah's Ark symbolises God's chastisement and mercy. The rainbow on its own symbolises God's mercy; also Hope. The dove and olive branch symbolise Peace.

The parable of the Good Samaritan.
Charity, benevolence, goodwill towards one's fellow men (see 'The virtues', see above).

Lamb and flag, Lamb and cross.
The Lamb symbolises Christ, and more generally innocence and humility.

The tablets of the Ten Commandments.
The moral law.

A dove flying downwards with wings outstretched.
The descent of the Holy Spirit.

Serpent.
The serpent has been a symbol of wisdom since Old Testament and Ancient Greek times. As the serpent renews itself by shedding its skin, it can also symbolise renewal and resurrection and has occasionally been used as a symbol of Christ. A serpent bent in a circle biting its own tail (the 'worm Ourobouros') is a symbol of eternity. The serpent does not usually signify wickedness in fraternal- and friendly-society symbolism except in the context of the Adam and Eve story.

Bees, Beehive.
The beehive shown is usually the traditional basketwork 'bee-skep'. Bees and beehives symbolise community and collaborative industry leading to prosperity.

Clasped hands (usually two, but occasionally four).
Mutual help and responsibility, reciprocal friendship.

A man trying to break a bundle of sticks (sometimes this image is expanded to include several onlookers; sometimes it is reduced to a bundle of sticks alone).
The strength of unity. This image derives from an ancient moral fable about a man who taught his sons the value of unity by making them break a single stick, which they could do easily, and then asking them to break a whole bundle of sticks tied together, which they found impossible. The classical Romans used the bundle of sticks, signifying strength in unity, as the symbol of their Republic, with an axe in the middle of the bundle; this symbol was called the *fasces*. It was adopted in 1920s Italy by Mussolini and gave its name to his political party – the Fascists.

A human eye with rays of light emanating from it.
This is a very widespread symbol, which has at least three possible meanings:
1) The All-Seeing Eye of God – this is its meaning in Freemasonry and, because of Masonic influence, probably also in most friendly societies.
2) (In Oddfellowship) Charity – a nineteenth-century Oddfellow handbook explains that the eye symbolised Charity because 'that alone can be true charity which is omniscient, and which can penetrate below the outward show of things. It also enjoins circumspection in character and discrimination in affording relief.'
3) (In continental Europe) Surveillance – for example, in France it is the badge of the Customs Service and in the United States that of the Pinkerton Detective Service.

Skeleton, Skeleton with scythe, Skull or skull and crossbones, Coffin (less common).
Death – an ancient symbol with multiple meanings. In many societies the

candidate member was brought in blindfolded, and when his blindfold was removed after the initiation ritual he found himself face to face with a figure of Death. This was done partly to give him a fright (a nasty shock is a stock feature of initiation rituals in cultures all over the world), but each society might give it one of a number of moral meanings, such as:

1) From classical times, as a memento mori (reminder of death). The memento mori was intended to point up moral thoughts such as 'life is short, prepare for your end'.

2) In initiation, to symbolise the death of the initiate's old self and his rebirth to a better and more enlightened life.

3) As a literal metaphor of the 'corporate' nature of human society, comparing the different members of the body to the different classes of society. Radical groups and trade-based societies such as the Tolpuddle Martyrs used the figure of a skeleton to illustrate the idea that, as society relied equally on all its members, they should all have equal rights, or enough pay to live on.

Crown, Crown on cushion, Sword and sceptre on cushion, Garter.
Loyalty to the Crown and the established order of society. This was often an important point to stress in the eighteenth and the first half of the nineteenth century, when fraternal societies were often suspected, sometimes correctly, of radical political activity. (However, the Garter could also be simply a convenient and conventional shape on which to display a motto.)

Time, shown as an old man with scythe and hourglass; sometimes just the hourglass, perhaps with wings.
A reminder of the shortness of life and the need to prepare for old age and death, both practically (by making provision for one's funeral expenses and dependants) and morally. The winged hourglass signifies that 'time flies'.

Astrological, astronomical and geometric symbols are common. They have many possible meanings, including the following:

Sun and Moon. Night and day.
Stars, usually seven. The Pleiades, sometimes the seven Liberal Arts. Sun, Moon and Stars together symbolise the heavens in general.
Zodiac symbols. The heavens; the course of the year; the wisdom of the ancients.
Globes, terrestrial and celestial. The whole of creation; or learning, education and understanding.
The Golden Section. This is an illustration of Euclid's forty-seventh theorem of geometry. It symbolises perfection, proportion, the 'golden mean'.

Tools are quite common. Sometimes they are simply the tools of the craft after which the society is named, but societies often invested them with moral significance also; for example, at face value the pruning knife is a gardening implement, but the Free Gardeners also read it as a symbol of moral self-improvement (the cutting out of one's bad impulses in order to allow the good to flourish). Because of the enormous influence of Freemasonry on fraternal symbolism, stonemasons' tools often appear in societies that have no obvious connection with stoneworking; these societies may have given them more or less the same meanings that they had in Freemasonry, or quite different ones.

Hammer, mallet, gavel. As the gavel is used to knock off unwanted parts of a stone, it represents control of the passions.

Set square. Defines the relation between the horizontal and the upright and thus represents a proper balance between different values and qualities.

Compasses. Signifies the need to draw appropriate limits – to 'keep within compass'.

Objects used in the ritual and furnishing of lodges are often depicted on items such as aprons. These may have many layers of meaning and may mean different things to different societies.

Temple. In Freemasonry this represents the Temple of Solomon, but it is used by other societies also.

Altar (with fire). The fire may signify the divine flame.

Pair of columns or pillars. In Freemasonry these symbolise the two pillars of Solomon's Temple, called Jachin and Boaz.

Chequered floor. Masonic lodges have a chequered floor or carpet – the 'drawing floor'.

Masks. A reference to initiation ritual. In the early initiation ritual of many of the older societies the members wore masks to frighten the initiate when his blindfold was removed.

Numerous plants appear with symbolic meaning:

Palm. In the Near East this was considered the tree of life. In Christianity it symbolises Christ's entry into Jerusalem, righteousness and peace. It also symbolised victory.

Laurel. Sacred to Apollo; symbolises immortality and victory. It was chewed by the Sibyl of Delphi to help her prophesy and so symbolises divination. Worn as a wreath, it symbolises poetry and excellence in the sciences and arts. With reference to the nymph Daphne it symbolises chastity.

Oak, Acorn. Sacred to pagan thunder-gods all over Europe, such as Jupiter and Thor. The oak was considered to be immune from lightning and therefore lucky and protective. It symbolises courage and strength; as 'Hearts of oak' it symbolises Britishness.

Rose. Symbolises the unity of England (the dynasties of Lancaster and York combined in the Tudor rose).

Thistle. The badge of Scotland: symbolises self-defence, as in the motto *Nemo me impune lacessit* ('No one provokes me with impunity').

Shamrock. The badge of Ireland: signifies the Holy Trinity, as expounded by St Patrick.

Leek. The badge of Wales: an attribute of St David, possibly because he ate leeks when living as a hermit, or possibly because he told Britons to wear them in their hats when fighting the Saxons. The daffodil is sometimes substituted because its name in Welsh means 'St Peter's leek'.

Even with a good knowledge of the symbolism used in this kind of material it is not always easy to interpret the meaning of the motifs used on any single object. Some of the possible sources of confusion are outlined here.

The mass-market manufacturers of regalia kept their prices down by using standard shapes with only a small space to add the individual society's emblem; thus most of the decoration on a cheap item might well be quite unrelated to that society.

Similarly, the Victorian taste for ornament often led makers to cover every surface with decoration, and, while motifs such as the rose, thistle and shamrock may have been meant to convey a serious patriotic meaning, it is often possible that they were simply a convenient way of filling a space.

On breast jewels in particular some symbols may relate to the individual lodge rather than the order. For example, the presence of a prancing horse on a Druid jewel may seem puzzling – what have horses to do with Druid lore? – unless we know that the jewel is that of a Kentish lodge, and that the prancing white horse is the badge of Kent.

Most societies have characteristic 'emblems' or assemblages of symbols, but these are rarely completely consistent. It is quite common for the details of an emblem to vary over time, or between one manufacturer's products and another; the colours of a heraldic shield may not be consistent, or the motifs on a quartered shield may vary in position. Elements of the design may be added or subtracted according to the size of the item being decorated – printed certificates allow for very elaborate detail, whereas small items such as lapel pins can show only the most important elements. With societies that were split into many different groupings, for example the Oddfellows, it is often hard to be sure if one is looking at the emblems of two different societies or at two different versions of the same emblem.

The Freemasons

Freemasonry is the best-known of all the fraternal organisations; indeed it is the only one that many people have heard of. From a small beginning it now comprises more than nineteen separate orders in the United Kingdom alone; it is because of this diversity rather than its place as the largest present-day fraternity that this chapter is so large.

The precise story of the origins of Freemasonry are obscure but it seems to have begun in England in the late seventeenth century, when scholars and intellectuals such as Elias Ashmole, the founder of the Ashmolean Museum in Oxford, joined stonemasons' lodges as 'speculative' masons, meaning that they did not actually do any stone-cutting but used the tools of the stonemasons allegorically to point moral lessons, and developed ritual morality plays around the biblical story of the building of Solomon's Temple at Jerusalem. In 1717 four London lodges held a feast at the Goose and Gridiron tavern in the City of London and proclaimed themselves to be the premier Grand Lodge; this was the first organised Masonic body in the world. The ceremonies were combined with food and drink, and two, later three, ritual dramas (termed 'Masonic degrees') were developed. Because the ceremonies related to stonemasons and their tools they were known as the 'craft degrees' and Freemasonry is sometimes referred to as 'the craft'.

The Freemasons: Premier Grand Lodge apron, c.1780.

The Freemasons: Antient Grand Lodge apron, c.1780.

Below: *The Freemasons: Royal Arch regalia as worn in the twenty-first century.*

In 1751 a group of Irish masons in London, finding that they could not gain access to existing lodges, set up the 'Atholl' or 'Antient' Grand Lodge in competition with them. They claimed to have Masonic rituals purer and older than those of the premier Grand Lodge, whom they con-temptuously dubbed 'The Moderns'. The Antients extended the ritual with a new degree called the Holy Royal Arch. The premier Grand Lodge was forced to adopt this in turn but kept it separate from the three craft degrees by creating a separate order called the 'Supreme Grand Chapter'. The Antients were predominantly Chris-tian in outlook and, among other ceremonies, also created the Masonic Knights Templar.

In 1813 the two Grand Lodges amalgamated to form the United Grand Lodge of England, which continues to be the ruling body for all members of the first three or 'Craft' degrees of regular English Freemasonry, with a closely linked body – Supreme Grand Chapter – controlling the Royal Arch. All the

Regalia of a Past Master of Craft Freemasonry, c.1930. 'Freemason' is a shortening of the medieval term 'freestone mason'. Freestone masons were the most skilled of all stonemasons; they carved 'freestone', cut from the quarries by ordinary stonemasons, into finished blocks and sculptures. This model of skilled craftsmanship is the basis of Masonic symbolism.

other orders in England and Wales are independent bodies. Regalia and the ritual morality plays were standardised and the lodge room assumed its elaborate form. The Royal Arch was retained as a separate but closely linked order, its rulers being the same as those of the 'craft'. Its regalia of sash and apron were based around the colours of hangings in Solomon's Temple.

The new Grand Lodge removed all specific references to religion in its ritual and thus was able to initiate all 'men of good character who believe in a Supreme Being'. God was dubbed 'The Great Architect of the Universe'; by this device all religions represented in a lodge could interpret the rituals and prayers through their own faiths. The additional ceremonies and orders that had grown up in the Antient Grand Lodge were allowed to die or were actively suppressed as the United Grand Lodge of England established its identity.

The three ceremonies that introduce a man to craft Freemasonry each have a distinctive apron. After the first degree – initiation – the man becomes an 'entered apprentice' and wears a plain lambskin apron. After the second 'passing' he becomes a 'fellowcraft' and has an apron with sky-blue rosettes at the lower corners. Finally, on 'raising', he becomes a Master Mason and his apron and its flap are edged with sky-blue ribbon, with a third rosette on the flap. This apron also has two tassels on sky-blue ribbons. If this Mason goes on to become the master of his lodge the rosettes are replaced by silvered 'T'

A Masonic craft lodge room.

shapes. (Earlier examples of these aprons frequently appear slightly green because of the way the dyes in the ribbon age.)

The lodges are set out around a chequered carpet. The three senior lodge officers – the master and the senior and junior wardens – each have a throne, a pedestal and a candlestick, and they sit on the east, west and south sides (though these orientations are sometimes only symbolic). The tools of the stonemason are used, and at all times the set square and compasses are displayed on the 'Volume of the Sacred Law' on the master's pedestal. The moral lessons explored in the ceremonies are also the subject of lectures, and these each have a picture associated with them that is displayed on a large board known as a 'tracing board' (from early times when the diagrams would literally be traced in chalk on the floor of the room).

Officers of the lodge wear broad ribbon collars with their badges (jewels) of office hung from them. Jewels are also given traditionally to founders and past masters of lodges. These can be very ornate and have designs that reflect the identity of the lodge. Charity and commemorative jewels are also worn, the most commonly found being those for the Royal Masonic Institution for Boys (RMIB), the Royal Masonic Institution for Girls (RMIG) and the Royal Masonic Benevolent Institution (RMBI). Jewels were also issued to fund the Royal Masonic Hospital, the building of Freemasons' Hall and in commemoration of Royal and Masonic anniversaries.

Once a man has been the master of a lodge further promotion is possible, and the regalia for senior ranks is in dark blue and gold. Each Province (the old English counties) and overseas District can award these ranks and, in addition, there are national honours known as 'Grand Ranks' – these have a collar with gold embroidered leaves, edged with gold lace. The rulers of the organisation have aprons richly embroidered around the border in gold with pomegranates, lotuses and, for the Grand Master, ears of wheat. Serving Grand Officers wear collar chains.

Freemasons' jewels. Above: Charity and commemorative jewels: (from left to right) Golden Jubilee of Queen Victoria; Charity Steward jewel for the Royal Masonic Benevolent Institution; Bicentenary of Grand Lodge, 1917; Grand Lodge Charity jewel; Charity Steward jewels for the Royal Masonic Institution for Girls and Royal Masonic Institution for Boys; Diamond Jubilee of Queen Victoria. Far left: Past Master's jewel. (The hanging device is the 'badge' of the Past Master.) Left: Founder's jewel.

Grand Stewards at both provincial and national level have their aprons and collars in red with silver trimmings. They carry white wands of office.

The additional ceremonies and orders of Freemasonry devised by the Antient Grand Lodge were little practised from the creation of the United Grand Lodge of England until the death of His Royal Highness the Duke of Sussex, first Grand Master of that Grand Lodge. From that time onwards Masonic orders have developed continuously. These 'side' or 'additional' degrees have a far smaller membership than craft Freemasonry but they allow members to explore a wide range of moral issues through ritual. They are independent of the United Grand Lodge of England, but their members must first join the basic craft Freemasonry.

The largest grouping of these orders is administered from Mark Masons' Hall in London. Mark Masonry has similar regalia to those of the craft but with a red edging. Its badge is a building keystone decorated with symbols, and members have a 'Mason's mark' as a form of identity; this must be composed of straight lines as though chiselled into a stone. The ritual play for Mark Masonry involves the building of Solomon's Temple and the keystone features in it. Mark Masonry seems to have existed since the eighteenth century but was little practised from 1813 until the order was revived.

The Royal and Select Masters, sometimes termed the 'cryptic degrees', are a small order that developed out of Mark Masonry, finally obtaining distinctive triangular aprons in the 1920s.

The Royal Ark Mariners have a ritual based around the biblical story of Noah and the Flood; their costume has a rainbow decoration and their members wear a breast jewel depicting the rainbow and a dove. The order first existed in the late eighteenth century but was extinct by the 1830s and was revived only with the growth of the side orders in the late nineteenth century.

The Masonic Knights Templar and Knights of Malta explore morality through rituals based around chivalric quests. These orders are Christian in

The Freemasons: Grand Master's apron.

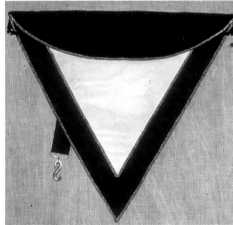

Freemasons' aprons: (above) Mark Mason; (right) Royal and Select Masters; (below) Royal Ark Mariner.

A Masonic Knight Templar, 1920s.

nature and the Templars were the final or *ne plus ultra* degree in the Antient Grand Lodge. They do not have any link to the actual historical Templars or to the Catholic order of the Knights of Malta. They have elaborate regalia – a medieval-style tabard and cloak worn with a cap and a sword. Rank is shown by neck jewels and the style of badge worn on the cape. In the 1800s an apron was worn rather than the tabard. Knights Templar meet in preceptories and Knights of Malta in priories.

The final order based at Mark Masons' Hall is the Order of the Secret Monitor. Imported from the United States, it uses the biblical story of David and Jonathan to explore brotherly love and sacrifice. The main item of regalia is a sash and certain grades wear swords.

The Ancient and Accepted Rite, sometimes known as the 'Scots Rite', is a thirty-three degree Masonic system used in the United States and France, among other countries. It admits only Trinitarian Christians, and in the United Kingdom it practises only a limited number of ceremonies representing the eighteenth and twenty-ninth to thirty-third degrees, with the other levels being conferred in name only. The entry level is the 'Knight of the Pelican', whose regalia include the crown of thorns and the cross on a collar with a jewel of the 'Pelican in its Piety'. This order previously wore an apron and sword. Higher levels of the order wear sashes and collars and their jewel is a two-headed eagle with rank indicated by the colours of the wing and tail feathers.

Members of the Order of the Secret Monitor, one of the orders based at Mark Masons' Hall, c.1890.

The remaining regular Masonic orders are small in membership and their regalia are rarely encountered. They include such orders as the Royal Order of Scotland, the Operative Masons and the Allied Masonic Degrees.

Each of the orders detailed above has distinctive room fittings for its ceremonies. Their regalia are normally found along with craft regalia, since anyone belonging to any of these side orders would own both. A useful guide to the smaller orders is the book *Beyond the Craft* (see 'Further reading').

Freemasonry is often thought to be a 'secret' activity; but from its early years until the beginning of the twentieth century Masons in full regalia were often

The Freemasons: Regalia of the Ancient and Accepted Rite.

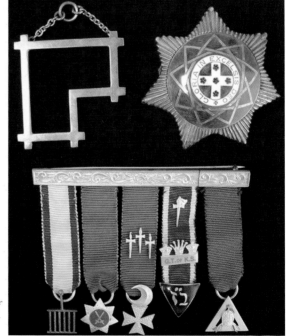

Members' jewels of some other Masonic side orders.

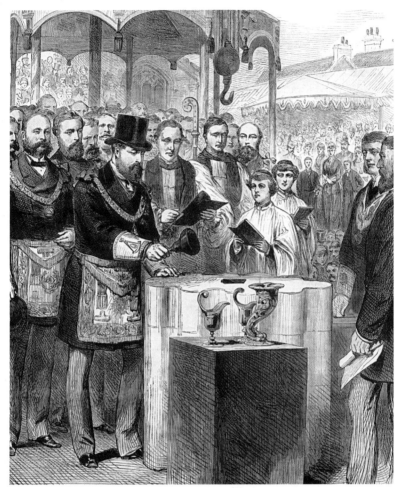

The Prince of Wales (later Edward VII), as Grand Master laying the foundation stone of Truro Cathedral. The impressive ceremonial and high social status of the Masons made them an obvious choice to undertake the laying of foundation stones at important buildings. The gold vessels in the foreground contained oil, wine and wheat; they are still used today in the consecration of Masonic lodges.

seen in public, for instance in such ceremonies as processions or foundation-stone layings. Although the actual ritual of Masonic meetings has always been secret, there was no mystery over who was or was not a Mason. However, in the 1920s and 1930s this changed, partly because Grand Lodge began officially to discourage Masons from displaying their membership in public, and possibly also because of nervousness caused by the rise of Fascism and Nazism on the Continent. (Both these movements were deeply opposed to Freemasonry and other fraternal societies; during the Second World War, when the Germans occupied a country they routinely seized the records of the Masonic Grand Lodges and used them to round up and arrest leading Masons.) Ever since then Freemasonry has featured very little in public life in Britain.

Jewel from a Co-Mason lodge.

Freemasonry is international, but each Grand Lodge is an independent body. Ireland and Scotland have their own Grand Lodges, and their regalia are different to those of the English and Welsh lodges controlled by UGLE. Only those that conform to certain strict rules known as the 'Ancient Landmarks' are recognised by the United Grand Lodge of England, and these are termed 'regular' Grand Lodges. Many other 'irregular' Masonic bodies exist across the world, but although to an outsider's eye they appear very similar they are not regarded as Masonic by the lodges in amity with English Freemasonry. Some of these bodies are ruled irregular because they are politically active or do not require belief in a deity; others admit women. None of these is acceptable to regular Freemasonry.

Female freemasonry has existed for more than a hundred years; in 2005 there were two

A female Mason, 1930s.

A Scottish Master Mason's apron.

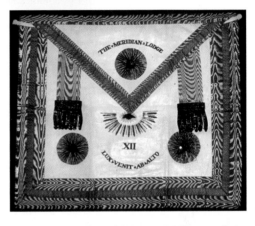

An Irish Master Mason's apron.

women's Grand Lodges in England, the Order of Women Masons and the Honourable Fraternity of Ancient Freemasons. In addition there are the 'Co-Masons', who have regalia very similar to that of Craft Freemasonry but with an orange border to their ribbons and all devices in gilt rather than silver, and the Grand Lodge of Freemasonry for Men and Women. Both of the two last-named orders admit both men and women.

Some English Masons have also belonged to the Scottish or Irish constitutions. Their regalia are similar to those of England, but in Scotland the apron has a circular flap and the colour varies from lodge to lodge, sometimes even being trimmed with tartan; Irish aprons have a distinctive line of metal braid laid in the middle of the ribbon edging.

This diversity and their long history means that of all the organisations in this book the Freemasons have had the largest body of material made for their members to use, wear or collect.

The Royal Antediluvian Order of Buffaloes

The Royal Antediluvian Order of Buffaloes (RAOB) is one of the largest remaining fraternal organisations in the United Kingdom. It is not a benefit society; it emphasises moral lessons, charitable giving and conviviality. Unlike many similar organisations, its origins are fairly certain: it grew out of a meeting at the Harp Tavern in Covent Garden, London, in August 1822 held by two stage artists as a protest against their exclusion from a stage guild known as the City of Lushington. Initially the organisation was purely social and its regalia and ceremonies deliberately frivolous, with the initiatory degree being the Kangaroo degree; even its name was derived from a music-hall song, 'Chasing the Buffalo'.

This early beginning was in contrast to what followed. By 1866 enough Buffalo lodges existed in London and elsewhere, perhaps spread by the theatrical profession, to justify the creation of a Grand Lodge. The original ritual seems to have been changed at that time to give the ceremonies more gravity. The structure of the Grand Lodge was modelled on the Masonic structure, with provincial Grand Lodges and subordinate lodges and chapters within them. The regalia also followed the Masonic model.

The lodge symbolically took the form of a city; the Master was referred to as Mayor, and the senior officers were Aldermen. Lesser officers carried the prefix 'City' in their title, for example City Taster, City Barber, City Physician.

The order was originally the 'Loyal' Antediluvian Order of Buffaloes, reflecting the need to emphasise its non-political nature, but this changed over time to the common usage 'Royal'. Permission to use this title was confirmed

Group photograph of a lodge of the Royal Antediluvian Order of Buffaloes, 1920s.

Directory of the Grand Lodge of England of the RAOB, 1957.

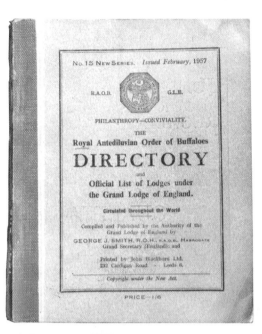

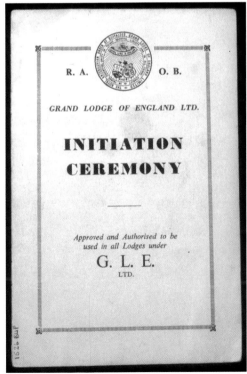

Printed ritual for the initiation ceremony of the RAOB.

Apron of the first or Kangaroo degree of the RAOB.

in the early 1900s when the Lord Chancellor declared it to be 'of common usage', although the order has no Royal Charter, which is normally a requirement for any organisation calling itself 'Royal'. The order continues to use the prefix 'Royal' by consent only. The word 'Antediluvian', which literally means 'from before Noah's Flood', was presumably chosen to go one better than other societies, who described themselves merely as 'Ancient'.

There are four levels of membership in the Buffaloes:

First degree or Kangaroo degree: the apron has a scene with two kangaroos on it.

Second degree or Certified Primo: conferred on the head of a lodge. This degree is awarded on the basis of long membership, consistent attendance and an examination on the ability to take the chair of a lodge.

Sash of the third or Knight Order of Merit degree of the RAOB.

72

*Regalia of the Royal
Antediluvian Order of
Buffaloes, Roll of
Honour degree:
(above) gauntlets;
(left) apron; (below
left) chain-collar;
(below right) sash.*

Third degree or Knight Order of Merit (KOM):
   wears red regalia.
Fourth degree or Roll of Honour (ROH): wears
   sky-blue regalia.

The third and fourth degrees are awarded for
commitment and attendance; members meet in
a chapter rather than a lodge. Promotion to a
provincial rank is also by virtue of service and
attendance. The provincial and grand officers
wear sashes embroidered with their ranks;
these are in a two-coloured diamond pattern.

The regalia remain elaborate to the present
day, with aprons, sashes and gauntlet cuffs, and
neck-chains for the two senior levels of Knight
Order of Merit and Roll of Honour. The custom
continues of wearing large numbers of jewels
to indicate membership of a lodge, the passing
of the degrees of membership and as
commemorative items.

An RAOB breast jewel.

Sash of the Grand Executive Banner of the RAOB.

Six RAOB breast jewels.

RAOB membership certificate, dated 1942. The scene to the lower right shows Queen Elizabeth I, who, according to RAOB legend, was 'the only Buffaloess in history'.

There are several distinct Grand Lodges or 'Banners', the largest of which is the Grand Lodge of England (GLE), based in Harrogate. These developed from splits in the order, creating among others the Grand Surrey Lodge, the 'Mother Lodge of the World'.

There is a parallel women's organisation, which meets in 'glades' rather than lodges. It is headed by a Grand Prima and, logically, has Dames rather than Knights of Merit.

The Knights of the Golden Horn

The Knights of the Golden Horn originated in the nineteenth century within the Royal Antediluvian Order of Buffaloes. The organisation seems originally to have had just one lodge, or 'encampment', the Hull Encampment, tasked with the running of ceremonies and the raising of members to the senior position of Knight of the Order of Merit.

In 1880 a group of Buffaloes met at the Robin Hood Hotel, Commercial Street, Middlesbrough, to discuss how to improve the Order of Buffaloes and make it more select. They decided that the answer was to expand the Knights of the Golden Horn as a higher order within the Buffaloes, and accordingly they applied for a charter from the Hull Encampment to open a new lodge on this altered basis. Permission was granted, and No. 1 Erimus Encampment opened in Middlesbrough on 22nd September 1880.

The new order spread rapidly in north-east England; by 1889 there were five more encampments, at Bradford, Wakefield, Huddersfield, West Hartlepool, and Stockton. All were subject to the rulings of the Hull Encampment and paid quarterly fees to it. There were three degrees: Companion, Knight Commander, and Order of the Shield.

All went well for several decades and the order continued to expand within the RAOB; however, eventually friction began to develop between the various districts and the Hull Encampment. The districts wanted to pass new by-laws to suit their individual circumstances, and the Hull Encampment continually

Apron of a Knight of the Golden Horn, matching the gauntlets (see page 36).

Neck-chain of the Order of the Shield, the third degree of the Knights of the Golden Horn.

Velvet collar of a Knight Commander of the Golden Horn.

Lodge jewel of the Novocastria Encampment (Newcastle) of the Knights of the Golden Horn.

vetoed them. In particular, the encampments wished to initiate new members, who were not Buffaloes, as Comrades of the Knights of the Golden Horn; this the Hull Encampment refused to allow. Finally, in 1926, the encampments sent a deputation to Hull to plead their case, which was rejected; they then decided to sever the connection with the Hull Encampment (and therefore with the Buffaloes) and form a new independent order, to be known as the Grand United Order of the Knights of the Golden Horn (GUOKGH).

The Hull Encampment seems to have withered away subsequently, and other bodies such as the Roll of Honour and Knights' Chapter arose within the RAOB to fulfil what had been its role. But the new independent GUOKGH flourished, still primarily in the north-east, and continues until the present day. There have been a total of 144 encampments opened within the order since 1880, some ten of which were still functioning in 2005. In spite of the break with the RAOB there does not appear to have been any hard feeling between the Golden Horn and the Buffaloes; it was acceptable to belong to both, and the RAOB museum contains displays of Golden Horn jewels and regalia.

The Knights of the Golden Horn were conceived as an order of chivalry, based on the knights of the First Crusade who went to the Holy Land via Constantinople and crossed from Europe into Asia there; the name derives from the inlet of the Bosphorus, called the Golden Horn, around which the city of Constantinople was built. (This may have been a riposte to the Masonic Order of Knights Templar; clearly any order of knighthood formed there would have had seniority over the Knights Templar, who were formed only after the Crusaders had captured Jerusalem.) The imagery and titles are in accordance with this concept – Grand Knight Commander, Scribe, and so on – as are the motifs on the regalia, which include lances, armoured

Jewel of a delegate to the annual conference of the order of the Knights of the Golden Horn in 1925.

Past officer's jewel of the Grand United Order of the Knights of the Golden Horn, reverse (above left) and obverse (above right).

knights, helmets and hunting horns (though the hunting horn tends to look remarkably similar to the bugle-horn badge used by the Light Infantry and Light Cavalry of the British Army). But the overall shape of the aprons and chain-link collars of the order is generally similar to that of Buffalo regalia.

The Free Gardeners

This group includes several distinct orders, including the Ancient Order of Free Gardeners, the Order of Ancient Free Gardeners, the St Andrew's Order of Free Gardeners and the National United Order of Free Gardeners Friendly Society.

The Free Gardeners are one of the oldest of the friendly societies, possibly older than the Freemasons. Their origins can be traced back to seventeenth-century Scotland, an era in which the Scottish nobility and gentry began to take an interest in modernising and beautifying their houses and grounds, and laying out their gardens according to the aesthetic and often symbolic principles formulated on the Continent during the Renaissance. This trend required new skills from a master gardener – a knowledge of modern ideas in garden design and the principles behind them, the ability to source exotic plants and seeds, and to manage and teach numerous apprentices and assistants. Thus the craft of gardening grew in importance, and master gardeners needed to stay in contact with each other to exchange professional knowledge.

The earliest evidence of the existence of a lodge of gardeners is the minute book, now in the Scottish Records Office, of 'ye Fraternitie of the Gairdners of East Lothian', a body meeting in the town of Haddington. The first entry is dated 1676 and contains a list of fifteen rules. The Haddington gardeners were to help each other in their work and share new knowledge; not to speak ill of fellow gardeners to their employers; not to poach each other's apprentices or jobs. Provision was made for gardeners travelling in search of work. Fines were imposed for swearing and non-attendance at meetings, and the income from such fines was to be used for the support of widows, orphans and the poor of the fraternity.

Polychrome jug of the 'Free and Ancient Gardeners'.

The emblem of the Free Gardeners, in brass, possibly a desk ornament or a piece of lodge furnishing.

All this is much like the rules of a trade guild, or an 'incorporation', which was the Scottish equivalent; in the seventeenth century the burgh of Haddington had nine such incorporations. It is possible that the gardeners were not eligible to become an incorporation because most of them did not live and work actually within the town, as craftsmen such as the tailors, wrights and bakers did, and therefore chose another form of organisation. They may have modelled their rules on those of stonemasons' guilds, which because of the peripatetic nature of their trade

Membership certificate of a Jewish Scottish Free Gardeners' lodge.

had a lodge-based system more flexible than that of the town guild or incorporation.

One striking difference from the normal guild or trade confraternity is that from the beginning the Fraternitie of the Gairdners of East Lothian admitted gentlemen to membership, on payment of a higher fee. No doubt this was beneficial to the fraternity, by improving its finances and helping to legitimise it in local society (given that it had no other official status). It is less clear what the gentlemen gained from joining – possibly help in laying out and managing their gardens, and access to the plants and seeds that the gardeners imported; possibly they saw gardening as a vehicle for philosophical ideas just as intellectuals in England were adopting stonemasonry at about the same time. There must have been some benefit to them, as in the early 1700s another independent Lodge of Gardeners was formed in Dunfermline; among the signatories to its Bond of Union were two important noblemen, the Earl of Moray and the Marquis of Tweeddale.

Given the numbers of gentlemen who joined them, the meetings of these lodges presumably had some social and fraternal content as well as practical trade matters. Nevertheless, they continued to concern themselves with real gardening, and by 1772 the Haddington Lodge was holding biannual flower shows; indeed the gardeners' lodges are reckoned to have introduced the whole concept of flower shows into Scotland.

By the end of the eighteenth century at least three more lodges existed in Scotland, at Bothwell, Cambusnethan and Arbroath, and there is shadowy evidence of lodges in England also. In England they seem to have grouped themselves into some kind of association quite early in the nineteenth century; in 1842 a body known as the Order of Ancient Free Gardeners Lancashire Union split from an earlier body, whose name is unknown, over a refusal by the parent body to reduce the 'tramping allowance' of two shillings a day and to commit the ritual to print.

Before any Grand Lodges existed in Scotland, new lodges were formed by permission from other lodges; for example, during the Napoleonic Wars a lodge of Free Gardeners was formed in the Edinburgh militia by permission of a lodge in Berwick-upon-Tweed. This eventually was found unsatisfactory, and on 6th November 1849 a meeting was held at Lasswade, Midlothian, to which all known lodges were invited to form a Grand Lodge. At least twenty Scottish lodges existed at this time. By 1859 the need for better organisation became apparent and representatives from more than a hundred lodges attended a meeting in Edinburgh at which it was agreed to have a Western and an Eastern Grand Lodge. However, many lodges declined to join this system, and at least fifteen Free Gardeners' lodges continued to exist independent of any higher authority, including the ancient Dunfermline Lodge.

The early Gardeners' lodges, particularly the Dunfermline Lodge, attracted a large number of gentlemen and noblemen in the early eighteenth century but after that Gardenry lost ground to Freemasonry as an upper-class activity; this must have been partly because Freemasonry gave the entrée into a national and indeed international network, whereas the Dunfermline Lodge never sponsored daughter lodges but accepted members wherever they actually lived. Membership was thus of limited use to men not living in or near Dunfermline, who could not attend meetings regularly, especially as they did not have reciprocal membership of other lodges belonging to the two Grand Lodges of Scotland.

Various orders and independent lodges of Free Gardeners continued to operate as benefit societies, with a special interest in gardening, throughout the nineteenth century, but the National Insurance Act of 1911 and the First World War seriously depleted their ranks and no lodge is known to have been formed in Scotland after 1908. There was a revival between the world wars, but they died out gradually after the Bevin Act. But Gardenry remained strong in the West Indies and Australia, and in 2005 a few lodges still existed in the United Kingdom under the auspices of the Caribbean British Order of Free Gardeners.

In 2002 a group of Scottish Freemasons set up a Gardeners Preservation Society and created a new order, the Order of Free Gardeners, to maintain the traditions of Scottish Gardenry, which had become completely defunct. In 2004 there were already four lodges of this revived order in Scotland. It is a purely fraternal order, with no benefit aspect.

RITUAL

The Haddington minute books nowhere deal directly with ritual, but occasional indirect references to initiations and 'the words and signs' occur; the first of these is in 1726, but the lodge may well have had an initiation ritual from the beginning. From the scanty evidence it appears that the Haddington Lodge originally had only one initiation and thus one degree, but by the late nineteenth century the order had developed a system of three degrees – Apprentice, Journeyman and Master – equivalent to those in craft Freemasonry. A partial lecture exists that was written in 1873 and printed in 1908; the earliest surviving complete book of lectures is dated 1930. These texts show that the

Apron of the Ancient Order of Free Gardeners, in blue cloth with velvet flap and gold fringe, and hand-painted panel in the centre.

84

central idea of Free Gardenry was based on the images of gardening in the Old Testament, with occasional references to the New.

> Gardenery may be defined as the art of disposing the earth in such a manner as to produce whatever vegetables and fruits we desire…

> Free Gardenery is the applying of the cultivation of the ground and its productions as symbols expressive of the necessity of cultivating the mind in intelligence and virtue.

The first or Apprentice degree was based on the story of the Garden of Eden and Adam, the first gardener, in which God was described as 'The Great Gardener of the Universe'. When Adam fell from grace he put on an apron, just as the Free Gardeners wore one, and had to go forth into the world and battle with weeds, briars and thorns, the effects of his sin.

The second or Journeyman's degree related to Noah, the gardener who planted a vineyard after the Flood. It also speaks of the four rivers flowing out of the Garden of Eden described in chapter 2 of the book of Genesis: Pison, Gihon, Hiddekel (Tigris) and Euphrates.

The third or Master's degree is about Solomon, described as a gardener,

Two aprons of the Ancient Order of Free Gardeners, in blue cloth with velvet flap, gold fringe and applied gold braid.

Sash of the Ancient Order of Free Gardeners, in blue silk with printed silk panel, gold embroidery and bullion tassels.

presumably on account of the imagery of gardens in the Song of Solomon.

Other biblical references are used, to gardens such as Gethsemane, and a number of trees and plants mentioned in the Bible were given significance, especially the olive (sign of peace) and hyssop (a symbol of purification from sin).

VISUAL SYMBOLS

The earliest evidence of the visual imagery of the Free Gardeners is a stone dated 17th July 1754 marking the plot of the Greenock Gardners' Society, which shows a tree (perhaps intended as a Tree of Knowledge) flanked by a rake, a spade, a level and a skirret (a tool for marking out ground), all of which would have been used by working gardeners.

Sash of the Ancient Order of Free Gardeners, in blue velvet with gold embroidery and bullion fringe, and two padded satin stars.

A group of five silver breast jewels of the Ancient Order of Free Gardeners, each showing the emblem of the order – the square, compasses and pruning knife – in a different style.

Above left: *Past officer's jewel of the Ancient Order of Free Gardeners, in silver and dating from 1837. It was probably meant to be stitched to a collar.*

Above right: *Past officer's jewel of the Ancient Order of Free Gardeners, in silver with the emblem in gilt.*

Although the origins of Gardenry do seem to predate those of organised Freemasonry there is little doubt that its symbolism shows Masonic influences. The key symbol of the Gardeners is the square and compasses with the addition of a half-open pruning knife (whose purpose, according to the ritual books, was 'to cut away vices and engraft the virtues of brotherly love and affection').

Silver presentation medal of the 'Ancient Free Gardners', from 1861, with an engraving of Noah's Ark.

Jewel, possibly cupro-nickel, of the Loyal and Independent Gardeners, obverse (above left) and reverse (above right).

Other gardening tools – rake, spade, hoe, basket – make appearances, especially on large items such as banners. Banners and tracing boards often show a scene of the Garden of Eden.

The apron of the Ancient Order of Free Gardeners is similar in shape to that of Scottish Masons, with a semicircular flap. This may have been a case of imitation, but it is possible that the Gardeners' apron derives from that of a working gardener, just as the Masons adopted theirs from that of operative stonemasons. On the apron of a Master Gardener are a picture of Noah's Ark and three linked triangles in which are contained the letters 'A', 'N', 'S' and 'O'. The first three letters are the initials of the three Biblical gardeners named in the three degrees; the meaning of the 'O' in the centre is unclear. The letters 'PGHE' appear, these being the initials of the rivers Pison, Gihon, Hiddekel and Euphrates.

The Oddfellows

The Oddfellows are certainly one of the oldest of the friendly societies, but their early history is extremely obscure. Even the origin of their name is unknown and there are many legends accounting for it. One traditional explanation has it that they were the 'hod fellows' who carried stone for the medieval Masons; another that they were a mixed guild of journeymen ('fellow craftsmen') following different trades, who were not eligible to join the master craftsmen's guilds and therefore banded together in lodges of 'odd fellows'; yet another that the name was chosen to point up a contrast between their varied membership and that of the allegedly more exclusive Freemasons. The most extravagant legend traces their origins back to the exile of the Israelites in Babylon in the sixth century BC and claims that the order was brought to Europe by Jewish prisoners after the destruction of the Temple at Jerusalem by the Roman Emperor Titus in AD 70.

However, the earliest definite historical record of the Oddfellows is the manuscript of the Rules and other documents of the 'Loyal Aristarcus' Lodge No. 9 of the Order of Oddfellows, which met at inns in Southwark, Hatton Garden and Smithfield, dated 1748. At this time the order seems to have been a convivial society of a conventional Georgian type, evidently – given that there were presumably eight older lodges in existence – already well established. There are hints that it had been influenced by the Society of Gregorians. If this was its original character the name might simply have been a joke; there were many convivial societies in London with comical names, such as the Codheads, the Gang, the Friendly Batchelors and the Knights of the Brush. The membership seems to have been mainly from the tradesman class, although at the time of the Gordon Riots John Wilkes and Sir George Savile were members. It is not clear if the Oddfellows were an organised 'order' at that time – they may well have been quite independent lodges.

The Oddfellows seem to have had a fairly affluent membership around the turn of the eighteenth and nineteenth centuries, and at least into the first half of the nineteenth century they had lavish and exotic costumes. The Nottingham Oddfellows (founded in 1812) laid down in 1835 that the chairman or 'Grand Imperial' of a lodge should have a scarlet robe with crimson cords, collar and cap, and yellow silk or gold trimmings; the 'Vice-Grand' was to have blue trimmed with white silk or silver; the 'Imperial Father' a black gown, belt and hat with scarlet collar and facings, and the Secretary a green robe with scarlet facings, collar and turban. Ordinary members were to wear green velvet turban caps and green velvet collars with white borders; in addition past officers were to wear sashes of various colours. A Nottingham Oddfellow procession in the 1830s must have been quite a sight.

It is not clear when the nature of Oddfellowship changed from being a convivial society to a friendly society but this seems to have happened by the very early nineteenth century. By the end of the eighteenth century many of the lodges, originally all more or less independent, had joined together to form the Patriotic or Union Order.

According to the *Complete Manual of Oddfellowship*, published in London in 1879, the Patriotic Order in 1797 had five degrees – the Initiatory, Covenant, Royal Blue, Pink (or Merit) and Royal Arch of Titus (or Fidelity) – with signs, passwords, grips, oaths of secrecy and an elaborate ritual involving costumes, props, lighting and sound effects.

Four lambskin Oddfellows' aprons from the early nineteenth century. The one at the top has a characteristic double-curved flap, and the one centre left has a tartan ribbon. For some reason tartan ribbons are common on Oddfellows' regalia.

The Initiatory degree entailed an extensive preliminary ordeal. The lodge room was in darkness except for a single fire and was set up with a 'road' made of loose rough planks. The candidate was brought in naked, blindfolded and pinioned with two cords, and pushed and pulled along the 'rocky road', making three circuits of the lodge room. On the second circuit he was thrown off the road so as to fall among a pile of cork 'rocks'; on the third he was deliberately entangled in a 'forest' of bundles of brushwood. Then he was burned at a lit brazier and finally he endured a 'tempest', in which he was drenched by a shower bath while the assembled brethren shrieked, groaned and made thunder noises with a gong and shaken sheets of copper. Afterwards he was made to swear an oath while all these props were quietly removed; then the blindfold was removed to reveal the still-darkened lodge room with 'emblems of mortality', including a real skull and crossbones, and all the lodge members in fright masks. He was threatened with death for 'trespassing' but pardoned on the plea of his sponsors. He was given a sermon on the skull, then told to close his eyes while the death scene was removed, the lodge was re-lighted, and the brothers unmasked and 'resumed a placid appearance'.

Finally the initiate's nakedness was covered by a plain lambskin apron, which he was told symbolised both the covering with aprons by Adam and Eve of their lost innocence and the sacrifice of the Lamb of God atoning for the fault of Adam and Eve. He was told that his naked entry into the lodge room was emblematic of his birth; the two cords represented the impulses of good and evil.

Similar initiatory rituals are recorded for other groups of Oddfellows of the period. They differed in detail but were all evidently impressive and frightening, and – if performed with gusto – potentially painful as well. Such rituals must have acted as a powerful bond between the members, and it is easy to understand the nervousness of the government at the prospect of them being used by revolutionaries or trade unionists.

The 1797 Unlawful Oaths Act and the 1799 Unlawful Societies Act led to splits and secessions as the various orders and individual lodges of Oddfellows grappled with the question of whether to abandon all these rituals, tone them down, or carry on regardless. It is possible that many bodies of Oddfellows who abandoned the oath and rituals at that time later readopted them – or new ones – when the panic of Jacobinism and foreign invasion was over. It is recorded that at Sheffield in 1822 the Grand United Order of Odd Fellows codified and confirmed a set of signs, tokens and oaths of secrecy at a time when these were still wholly illegal.

Oddfellowship throve in the early nineteenth century as a friendly society, and the Manchester Unity began to establish itself as the leading branch of the Oddfellows movement (though it was never the only one). But the movement received a nasty shock in 1834 with the conviction of the Tolpuddle Martyrs under the 1797 Act. In a panic the Manchester Unity abolished its higher degrees, and the oaths of initiation to the remaining degrees were replaced by a simple promise.

Oddfellowship was already well established in North America by the beginning of the nineteenth century, and, as United States Oddfellows were not subject to the British legal sanctions against oaths and ritual, they continued to use them. It is possible that the extensive use in North American Masonic ritual of props, costumes, lighting and sound effects – something unknown in British Masonry – owes something to Oddfellow influence. The British and American Oddfellow movements parted company in the 1830s, partly because the American Oddfellows continued to use their rituals and indeed to add extra degrees, and partly because of a move by them to impose teetotalism, which the British movement had no wish for. However, after some years of separation articles of reciprocity between the British and United States movements were signed in 1850.

Oddfellowship in Britain was subject to continual splits and secessions. The *Complete Manual of Oddfellowship* stated that, as well as ten other minor orders, the most important groups of Oddfellows in Britain at that time were:

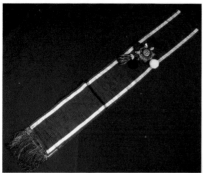

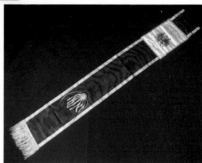

The Oddfellows: a series of three Manchester Unity sashes.

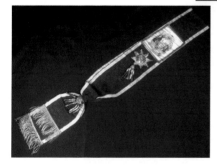

The Manchester Unity: formed by a secession from the Patriotic Order in 1813.

Grand United Order of Oddfellows: an early secession from the Manchester Unity. Rules certified in 1851.

Nottingham Ancient Imperial Order of Oddfellows: seceded from Sheffield Unity about 1812.

Ancient Noble Order of Oddfellows, or Bolton Unity: seceded from Sheffield Unity in 1832.

British United Order of Oddfellows: seceded from the Imperial Nottingham Order in 1867.

Improved Independent Order of Oddfellows, or London Unity: seceded from the Manchester Unity about 1820.

Albion Order of Oddfellows: seceded from the Manchester Unity at Nottingham in 1831. There were subsequently several secessions from the Albion Order – the Nottingham Independent Order, the Derby Midland Order, the Ilkison

The Oddfellows: a collarette of the Aristarcus lodge.

Unity, the Norfolk and Norwich Unity.

Kingston Unity of Oddfellows: seceded from the Manchester Unity at Hull in 1840.

National Independent Oddfellows: a group with Chartist sympathies, founded in Manchester and Salford in 1846 as a secession from the Manchester Unity.

Ancient Independent Order of Oddfellows, or Kent Unity: originally founded at Woolwich in 1805 but not very active until 1861, 'when the Britannia Lodge, as the mother lodge, began to issue dispensations'. Rules registered in 1871.

Wolverhampton Unity of Oddfellows: ceased to exist as a separate order in 1876, when it amalgamated with the Ancient Order of Shepherds.

The Oddfellows: a Manchester Unity apron with polychrome print.

In the nineteenth century Oddfellowship was exported to the colonies; it was and still is particularly strong in Australia. The Manchester Unity finally began to accept women members, initially in separate women's lodges and districts, after 1911 in order to qualify as an 'approved' society for National Insurance. Oddfellowship continued to thrive into the mid twentieth century and until the introduction of the state pension and the National Health Service. At least four orders of Oddfellows weathered the blow and were still functioning in 2005: the Manchester Unity, the Kingston Unity, the National Independent Order and the Grand United Order. They continue to offer social fellowship in lodges, as well as mutual financial services, and still wear regalia.

REGALIA

Oddfellowship had always used an extensive set of symbols, some specifically Christian, some of a generally moral nature. These symbols were employed in the instruction of candidates to the degrees of the Manchester Unity up to 1869, when the Unity abolished their use and replaced them with unexceptionable (and rather dull) lectures on Charity, Truth, Knowledge and Science. However, there seems to have been resistance to this move by the membership; the *Complete Manual of Oddfellowship* remarks that 'At the present day, however, many Lodges even of the Manchester Unity adhere to the older ceremonies, and practice them in conjunction with the Lectures officially promulgated.'

The symbols continued in use on regalia, however, even when they were no longer used in instruction. All the Oddfellow orders drew on a common stock of images for their characteristic emblems and tended to employ a similar style of regalia.

The Oddfellows: Grand Lodge of Kent apron, with metal set square pinned to the flap. This may be a mourning apron.

Early-nineteenth-century aprons were often hand-painted on white lambskin; later ones were generally made of white silk, trimmed in the colour of the degree (also in black, for mourning aprons, worn at Oddfellow funerals). The shape of the apron varied, as did that of the flap, although a double-curved flap is very characteristic. Ribbon rosettes were also often applied to the flap and/or the apron; silk or gold bullion tassels often hung from the flap.

But the wealth of the different orders and of the lodges within the orders varied; very simple home-made aprons were also worn and it is often impossible to identify which particular group of Oddfellows they belonged to.

In many cases the main surface of the apron was taken up by the emblem of the order. Early-nineteenth-century lambskin aprons are often beautifully painted and are very varied, but commercially printed silk made it practicable to devise elaborate emblems. These emblems, though different, illustrate the essential kinship of Oddfellow symbolism. A list of popular emblems follows.

A heart on an open hand: this is the most characteristic Oddfellow symbol and any object bearing it is fairly certain to be an Oddfellow item – no other friendly societies seem to have used it. It signifies friendship and that any act of kindness (the hand) is without merit unless accompanied by the proper impulse of the heart.

The terrestrial globe: denotes the universal spirit of benevolence in Oddfellowship.

Hourglass: signifies truth, the shortness of time, and the certainty of death. It teaches promptness in assisting those in need and in improving oneself in the practical virtues.

Apron of the Caledonian Order of Oddfellows.

Crossed keys: signify the security of the order, and the treasures laid up in Heaven for those who believe, 'where the moth does not corrupt, etc'. (On its own, as in other societies, it is a treasurer's badge.)

Beehive: illustrates 'justice as the reward of industry', and the prosperity of a society based on right, fitness and justice.

Lamb and flag: the emblem of faith, purity and humility.

Skull and crossbones: signifies mortality.

The Eye of Providence: the rayed eye, which in Freemasonry signifies the All-Seeing Eye of God, in Oddfellowship is associated with charity, for 'that alone can be true charity which is omniscient, and which can penetrate below the outward show of things. It also enjoins circumspection in character and discrimination in affording relief.'

Noah's Ark: signifies trust and safety.

The dove and olive branch: usually depicted with Noah's Ark, these are emblematic of peace and goodwill.

The standard emblem of the Independent Order of Oddfellows Manchester Unity consists of two short pillars on a plinth; on the left pillar is a shield with diagonal stripes in red and yellow (the arms of the City of Manchester); on the right pillar a quartered shield of Britain (Scottish lion, Irish harp, two quarters of English leopards). Between the pillars is a moral scene (for example, Britannia and savages, or the fable of Unity – a man getting his sons to break a bundle of sticks). Above this is a shield divided by a cross: in the top-left quarter is an hourglass; in the top-right quarter crossed keys; in the lower-left quarter a beehive; in the lower-right quarter a lamb and flag. There is a central escutcheon with a rose, thistle, shamrock, and sometimes a leek. Flanking the shield are figures of Faith (with cross), Hope (with anchor) and Charity (either a woman with children or a scene of the Good Samaritan). Below the shield there is sometimes a cornucopia and dove with olive branch, sometimes just fruits, foliage and, again, rose, thistle and shamrock. Above the shield is a globe with the word 'BRITAIN', surmounted by a heart on hand and surrounded by laurel sprays. Above all is the rayed eye. Individual elements of this emblem can vary, and it is often simplified or elaborated depending on the size of the artefact decorated.

The emblem of the Independent Order of Oddfellows Grand Lodge of Kent, or Kent Unity, was a quartered shield: in the top-left quarter was an open Bible; in the top-right were four clasped hands; in the lower-left an hourglass and scythe; in the lower-right a skull and crossbones. In the centre was an escutcheon with the heart-on-hand motif. The shield is supported by Faith (with cross) and Hope (with anchor). Below the shield is a scroll with the motto 'PEACE and GOODWILL TO ALL MEN'. Suspended from the scroll are (left) crossed keys within a laurel wreath and (right) a set square and clasped hands within a roped border. At the base are Charity (with children) and the rose, shamrock and thistle. Above the shield are Noah's Ark, a dove with olive branch and a rayed eye, flanked by crossed swords and crossed halberds. Over all appears the inscription 'GRAND LODGE OF KENT. INSTITUTED 1851. INDEPENDENT ORDER OF ODD FELLOWS.'

The emblem of the Caledonian Order of Oddfellows (COOF) showed a plinth, at the front of which is a shield divided by a cross. In the top-left quarter of the shield is a lamb and flag; in the top-right, scales; in the lower-left quarter a dove; in the lower-right a beehive; in the centre an escutcheon with a raised hand. On and around the plinth are several figures: a Woodland Native

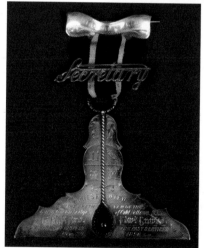

Five jewels of the Independent Order of Oddfellows South London Unity (IOOFSLU) – note the square and compasses: it looks Masonic but it is not.

A stylistic rarity – a 1912 Oddfellows Manchester Unity conference jewel in Art Nouveau style, with the 'MU' monogram in white and green.

American; a Turk; an African; a woman with children (Charity); a woman with spear and plumed helmet (Britannia or Fortitude?) and a female angel. Over all is a rayed eye.

The emblem of the Nottingham Ancient Imperial Order of Odd Fellows showed an architectural feature with pillars, bearing on the front a scene of the Good Samaritan. On the left pillar is a shield with a cross and three crowns; on the right pillar a shield with the arms of England. In front of the plinth are a crowned lion, a lamb, a dove with olive branch, and the motto 'UNITAS AMICITIA ET BENE-VOLENTIA' on a scroll. On the top of the plinth is a quartered shield; in the top-left quarter is an hourglass, in the top-right a skull and crossbones, in the lower-left a lion lying down, in the lower-right a lamb. In the centre of the shield is an open book; on the mid-line below the book is a heart on hand and on the mid-line above it is an eight-runged ladder. Round the shield is a garter with the motto 'HONOUR ALL MEN BUT SERVE THE BRETHREN'. Above this are a dove with olive branch on a heraldic wreath, the moon and stars in the sky, and above all a rayed eye. Flanking the shield are the figures of Faith (with cross), Hope (with anchor)

Early-nineteenth-century Oddfellows' mug. The three faces in the shield represent the masks used in the initiation ritual.

Cup and saucer of the Manchester Unity of Oddfellows.

and Charity (with children), as well as foliage, fruits, rose, thistle and shamrock.

The Nottingham Ancient Imperial Order of Odd Fellows eventually became the Nottingham Oddfellows Friendly Society, with a simplified emblem consisting of a dove and olive branch, and a shield on which are shown an hourglass, a ladder, skull and crossbones, an open book, a lion, a lamb, and a heart in hand. The motto remained 'UNITAS AMICITIA ET BENE-VOLENTIA'.

The Oddfellows seem to have had a taste for ceramics as well as regalia; in collections of 'Masonic' mugs and jugs it is commonplace to spot one bearing an Oddfellow emblem.

An American Oddfellows' jewel. The modern shirt and suit cuffs of the clasped hands are very characteristic of American Oddfellows – British Oddfellows never show these.

100

The Druids

The Ancient Order of Druids was founded in 1781 at the Old King's Arms Tavern in Poland Street, London, by a man named Hurle. Nothing is known about Hurle for certain, not even his Christian name, although he may have been a builder and surveyor based at Garlick Hill in the City of London. Druid tradition holds that Hurle was a member of the Bucks who found that order too rowdy and profane and decided to found his own fraternal order in which profane, political and immoral talk were forbidden. He may well have been a Freemason also, as the organisation and terminology of his order are heavily based on the Masonic model as well as on Druidical legend and symbolism.

Eighteenth-century British intellectuals were very interested in the Druids; they were attracted to the idea that ancient Britain had not been peopled by savages in mud huts but had an order of learning and wisdom that had rivalled – and possibly influenced – the Greek philosophers and the astrologers of ancient Persia. It was also believed that the Druids had believed in one all-powerful god and a prophesied redeemer; to the eighteenth-century mind this made them virtually proto-Christians, and therefore their rituals – or what were thought to be their rituals – could be revived and performed without any taint of paganism.

Hurle invented a colourful legend that his order had been founded by one Togo Dubellinus, the offspring of a secret marriage between a Druid priestess and a noble bard who was killed resisting the Roman invasion of Britain; their child was reared secretly in the forest by his mother until one day he was found

The King's Arms in Poland Street, Soho, in 2004, showing the commemorative plaque put up by the Ancient Order of Druids for their 150th anniversary in 1931.

The obverse (above left) of a Druid jewel dated 1811, with painted enamel scene of the finding of the infant Togo Dubellinus. The reverse of the jewel (above right), shows a Druid playing the harp.

in a hollow oak tree by a group of Druids seeking mistletoe. The infant was taken and brought up by the Druids and later became the most famous Archdruid of ancient times.

This story was a complete invention; neither the name Togo Dubellinus, nor the clandestine love story, nor the theme of a miraculous child found in an oak tree derives from anything in the classical literature that was all the eighteenth century knew about the Druids. Many of Hurle's early members (given that the public-school or grammar-school education of the time consisted mostly of the classics) must have known this, and one must wonder how seriously the first generation of his 'Druids' took it all. Nevertheless, this blend of antiquarianism, romance and Masonic-style ritual seems to have appealed strongly to Hurle's contemporaries, and his new order spread rapidly outwards from London, opening three lodges in the West Country in 1789 and 1790. Although many members of many early Druid lodges were clearly quite rich and could afford to commission beautiful and expensive jewels, its membership does not seem to have reached as far up the social scale as that of the Freemasons; lacking the Freemasons' royal and aristocratic support, they were not exempted from the Unlawful Societies Act of 1799. Some Druid lodges in Essex were prosecuted under the Act, and as in so many fraternal societies this led to a number of splits in the early nineteenth century.

The most significant split in the history of the Druid order came in 1833. From the beginning the Druids, like other eighteenth-century fraternal societies, had maintained charitable funds for which members could apply when in need. In 1833 a proposal was made to gain government approval and protection by becoming a registered friendly society, conforming to the government regulations for such societies, submitting to government audit, and offering fixed sickness, unemployment and other benefits to its members. The order split over this idea. Part of it continued as before, as an unregulated

The obverse (above left) of a jewel of the Druid 'Lodge of Harmony' in enamel and seed-pearls, 1807. (Above right) The reverse, with paste gems.

fraternal society, under the original title Ancient Order of Druids (AOD). The part that decided to become a registered friendly society became the United Ancient Order of Druids (UAOD). These two societies went their separate ways and both became enormously successful.

THE UNITED ANCIENT ORDER OF DRUIDS

The UAOD became one of the biggest of the benefit societies, alongside the Foresters and the Oddfellows. It acquired a strong membership in the colonies, where it formed an important support network for settlers; by 1895 it had 64,000 members worldwide, 25,595 of them in Australia alone. The UAOD called its lodges 'groves', in memory of the ancient Druids who had met in oak groves.

Like all the main benefit societies, towards the end of the nineteenth century the UAOD acquired juvenile lodges and began to admit women to membership, in segregated all-female lodges. The 1895 rulebook specified that, unlike men's lodges, female lodges might not meet in inns or pubs – by the late nineteenth century respectable women never drank in pubs, and the order was anxious to be impeccably respectable.

It developed a strong presence in the United States also, not only

Silver jewel with profile head of a Druid on blue enamel, 1830.

103

Silver jewel with the United Ancient Order of Druids emblem in gilt on a blue enamel centre, 1840.

among English-speaking settlers but among German and Scandinavian immigrants as well. Some of these immigrants returned home and took Druidism with them; by the end of the nineteenth century there were UAOD lodges in Germany and Scandinavia.

The UAOD maintained its prominent position among British benefit societies until the creation of the Welfare State after the Second World War, when it went into steep decline and was finally wound up in 1999 (though Commonwealth orders of the UAOD, long since independent of the parent body, in 2005 still had branches in the United Kingdom).

The emblem of the United Ancient Order of Druids was a shield with three trees of an odd three-lobed shape, encircled by a collarette with jewel,

Collar of a Past Arch of the UAOD, in green velvet with silver embroidered oak leaves and silver bullion fringe.

Collar of a Past Arch of the UAOD in red wool cloth, gold lace and gold fringe. The name of the owner has been unpicked, presumably for re-use.

Silver jewel of the UAOD with a gilt and enamel centre, 1852.

supported by a warrior with shield and spear and a robed figure with crook. The crest is a male head and torso holding a club in his right hand, and a similar tree in his left hand. The motto is 'UNITED TO ASSIST'.

THE ANCIENT ORDER OF DRUIDS

As a purely fraternal society – which entailed some expense on the individual members and did not absolutely guarantee any benefits – the AOD seems consistently to have had a more affluent membership than the UAOD. Certainly it continued the tradition of lavish individually produced jewels, and from an early date it also had an 'inner' order, the Royal Arch, just as Freemasonry did. The Royal Arch met in chapters rather than lodges, and its insignia included a silver triangle on a maroon neck-ribbon with the motto 'FRIENDSHIP / FIDELITY / OBEDIENCE', sometimes abbreviated to the initials 'FFO'.

Right: *Silver AOD jewel with profile head of a Druid, 1852.*

Below: *AOD jewel with a gilt central roundel under glass depicting a Druid playing the harp.*

As a fraternal society, the AOD was not under the same pressure to admit women as the UAOD was, and it remained a single-sex order.

Between the world wars the AOD's headquarters in London had the amenity of a plaster-of-Paris copy of Stonehenge, scaled down but still tall enough for a man to walk under the trilithons, for use in its ceremonies; this regrettably no longer exists. Not being a benefit society, the AOD was not affected by the welfare reforms of the 1940s in the same way as was the UAOD, but like all fraternal societies it suffered from changes in social habits and went into a decline. In 1989 it joined a 'Council of British Druid Orders' – an attempt to bring together different kinds of Druids, including the 'neo-pagan' groups – but this did not

Oval jewel with the AOD emblem in gilt and red foil under glass, 1886.

Above: *AOD Supreme Royal Arch Chapter jewel, 1888.*

Left: *AOD jewel with the head of a Druid in gold.*

prove fruitful and it left the Council in 1996.

The emblem of the Ancient Order of Druids was in the form of a shield with three three-lobed trees encircled by a collarette with jewel, supported by a warrior with shield and spear and a robed figure with crook. The crest was a male head and torso holding a club in his right hand and a three-lobed tree in his left. The supporting figures were not consistently on the same sides. The motto was usually in French – *Dieu, notre pays et Roi* (or *Reine*, in Queen Victoria's reign) – but sometimes in English – 'GOD, OUR COUNTRY & KING' (or 'QUEEN').

THE ORDER OF DRUIDS

The Order of Druids (OD) was a benefit society created by secession from the UAOD in 1858. Its emblem was a scene with a cornucopia, lamb, fasces, Celtic cross and corn-sheaf in the foreground; a row of shields

Group of four variants of the AOD Royal Arch Chapter jewel, one retaining its ribbon collarette.

Silk ribbon collarette of the Order of Druids; in the centre is a pressed base-metal ornament (a standard product) with the order's emblem in the centre.

with the national emblems of Britain, the United States, Australia and India in the middle ground; Stonehenge in the background; a Druid with a harp and a Celtic warrior flanking him and oak branches overhead. The Druid and the warrior point with crook and staff respectively to a roundel containing seven circles overlain by a triangle, with the motto 'INTEGRITAS PRO RUPE NOBIS'.

Between the world wars these three Druid orders considered themselves as sister organisations, with mutual membership and the right to attend each other's lodges – with the proviso that female members of the OD and the UAOD could not attend lodges of the AOD, which did not admit women. A congress of the three orders was held annually.

Apart from these three main orders, at any time since the early nineteenth century there were always smaller Druid fraternal or benefit societies. Some of these may have started up independently (Hurle's order was not the first 'Order of Druids' to be created in the eighteenth century), but most were splinters from one of the main groups. At times there were as many as thirteen friendly or fraternal Druid orders existing simultaneously (as distinct from the 'cultural' Druids of the Welsh eisteddfod movement, or the 'mystical' Druids celebrating the solstice on Primrose Hill or at

Jewel of the OD, possibly originally stitched to the centre of a collar or collarette. It is a standard George Tutill base-metal shape with the order's emblem in the centre.

Membership certificate of the Order of Druids.

Stonehenge), so it is often difficult to identify an item as belonging to a specific order unless the name of the order is inscribed on it. After the Second World War these groups gradually began to merge back together as their funds and membership numbers fell. In 2003 only two registered Druid friendly societies survived in Britain: the Sheffield Independent Druids and the Druids Sheffield Friendly Society (actually based in Rotherham). In that year the Independent Druids decided that the word 'Druids' projected the wrong image for a twenty-first-century savings society and re-branded themselves as the Sheffield Mutual Friendly Society, thus leaving the Druids Sheffield Friendly Society – itself created by the reunification of several different societies – as the sole representative of this great British tradition. In 2005 its officers were still wearing traditional regalia.

Jewel commemorating the 1933 Druidical Congress in London. These congresses were held annually and brought together the three main Druid orders.

These AOD jewels show how similar forms were used across different societies. The enamelled AOD cipher on the left-hand jewel is similar in style to that on the Buffalo jewel on page 75, and the star and wreath shape of the other is almost identical to that of the Phoenix jewel on page 23. However, the suspension bars are distinctively Druidical.

ARTEFACTS

The various groups of Druids in the nineteenth century used a full range of regalia and jewels, in a wide variety of styles and degrees of lavishness, and usually looked much like members of any other fraternal society.

Until 1891 the AOD wore aprons; after that date they abandoned them and kept the sash, collar and jewels only. In the early twentieth century some officers wore white robes and even false beards for their ceremonies, giving them a distinctive look. In 1908 Winston Churchill was initiated into the AOD at Blenheim and the *Oxford Times* printed a photograph of him surrounded by

AOD lambskin apron (pre-1891, as aprons were not worn in the AOD after that date).

Two jewels of a Past Noble Arch with the AOD monogram in red, white and blue enamel.

his new lodge brothers, some in chains and collarettes, some in robes and Father Christmas beards.

Druid lodges and chapters were headed by a Noble Arch Druid; this generally appears on jewels or regalia as 'NAD' or simply 'NA'. A Past Arch Druid was referred to as a 'PA'. (The founder of the Druids is usually referred to in Druid writings simply as 'P. A. Hurle', which makes it look as though his initials were 'P. A.' but in fact is an abbreviation of his official title. His real initials are unknown.) Other officials were Vice-Archdruid, Guardian, Bard, Director of Ceremonies, Secretary and, sometimes, Minstrel.

Druids, like many other groups, liked to commission ceramic items, both for use at lodge festivities and for personal use, and examples exist made by many of the leading British ceramic factories of the late eighteenth and the nineteenth centuries.

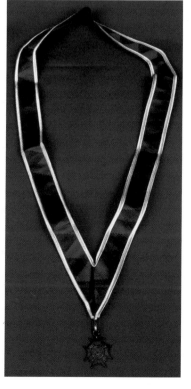

Grand Lodge of England jewel – bronze on silk ribbon collarette edged with gold braid.

Druid collarette with silver jewel inscribed 'B.G.P.' (Board of General Purposes?).

SYMBOLS

All the Druid orders shared a range of symbols relating to Druidism; the most common are detailed below.

Togo Dubellinus, Tau Delta cipher. The scene of the finding of Togo Dubellinus is rarely found on jewels and regalia – being too elaborate to depict in metal – but can appear on lodge certificates. The Tau Delta cipher (the Greek letters 'T' and 'D') was often used on AOD jewels but may have been used by other Druid groups also.

Druid. By the end of the eighteenth century the Druid had already been established in the popular mind by engravings in books on history and antiquities as an old man with a long

Right: *Sash of the AOD Royal Arch Chapter, apparently home-made, in thin silk and embroidered in silk with the initials 'FFO' for 'Friendship, Fidelity, Obedience'.*

Eighteenth-century creamware mug with a printed decoration of the 'Grand Lodge of Druids'.

Two Druid jewels with the Greek monogram Tau Delta (the initials of Togo Dubellinus).

white beard wearing white robes and a hood. The fraternal Druid orders drew on these images; thus artefacts from different Druid orders often depict near-identical figures. In many cases a simple head and shoulders in profile or a full face was all that was shown; this was clearly felt to be enough to convey the identity of the figure. When shown in full length the Druid was often depicted playing the harp, or holding a crook and/or a sprig of mistletoe.

Oak tree, Oak leaves, Acorns. The word 'druid' contains the Celtic word 'dru', meaning 'oak', and the classical writers described Druids as meeting and performing their rites in oak groves.

Mistletoe. Mistletoe was also important in Druid ritual, according to the classics.

Stonehenge. The historical Druids had nothing to do with Stonehenge and the other megalithic monuments of Britain, which date from a much earlier culture. However, ever since the antiquarian John Aubrey suggested in the seventeenth century that stone circles were built by Druids the two have been associated in the popular mind, and images of Stonehenge, or sometimes simply a single trilithon, often featured in Druid imagery and Druid ritual.

Crooks. Crooks were carried as symbols of office by lodge officers in at least some of the Druid orders. (They were called 'crooks' – by the AOD at least – but were meant to represent a long-handled sickle for cutting mistletoe rather than a shepherd's crook.) A pair of crossed crooks appears often on jewels, and sometimes the figure of the Druid is shown holding one.

AOD cipher. Jewels of the AOD were often decorated with the letters 'AOD' entwined monogram-style, very often in red, white and blue enamel.

Triangle. In addition to its usual significance, the triangle in Druidism symbolised fire (supposedly triangles look like flames). It is also the shape of the Greek letter delta, and so forms part of the Togo Dubellinus cipher.

Zodiac symbols. Its use in Freemasonry made the zodiac a popular feature in friendly and fraternal societies generally, but in Druidism it may also have referred to the belief that the astrologers of ancient Mesopotamia got some of their learning from the Druids.

The Ancient Order of Foresters

The Ancient Order of Foresters (AOF) is one of the oldest friendly societies, with its origins in Yorkshire. The earliest verifiable evidence of the Foresters' existence is in 1790, for which date a list survives of the members of Court No. 1 of the Order, which met at the Old Crown Inn in Kirkgate in Leeds. (In Forestry the word 'court' is used instead of 'lodge'; the metaphor is of the law courts of the royal forests, which since the Middle Ages had met to administer the special forest laws.) This inn was also the meeting place of the Masonic Lodge of Fidelity, and several members of this lodge were also members of Court No. 1, the first on the list being John Smithson of Knaresborough, from a well-known Quaker family. It is not known how long this court had already been in existence; there are hints that a group called the Royal Foresters had been meeting in Knaresborough in 1745, but no definite evidence survives, and even if it had, it would not necessarily mean that the two groups were directly connected.

In 1813 a Court No. 2 was established in Knaresborough; gradually more courts were opened. Court No. 1 renamed itself the Supreme Court of Antiquity in 1815 and became the controlling body of the order; this court is documented until it ceased to exist in 1858.

At this time the society was called the Royal Ancient Order of Foresters (RAOF); it is presumed that the word 'Royal' was derived from the Royal Forests, of which Knaresborough was one. Philanthropy and virtue featured prominently in the principles and ritual of the society: 'The object of Forestry is to unite the virtuous and good in all sects and denominations of man in the sacred bonds of brotherhood so that while wandering through the Forest of this World they may render mutual aid and assistance to each other.' Like Freemasonry, Forestry was open to anyone believing in a Creator. Just as its lodges were called courts, the officers of the society used the titles of officials of the medieval forest courts, such as Ranger and Woodward. However, the order blended this medieval idea with the notion of Adam as the first Forester. A pamphlet dated 1847 in the British Museum states that 'Forestry claims antiquity from Adam whose disobedience of the Commands of the Almighty brought upon himself his expulsion from the ever-blooming Gardens of Eden into the rude, uncultivated forests of the world', and describes how Adam made himself a club to defend himself from wild animals. It is notable that the date of the dispensation for the formation of Court No. 1 in 1813 was given as 'in the year of Forestry 5817' – this calculation is based on the nineteenth-century belief that God had created the world (and Adam, the first Forester) in 4004 BC.

In the early years of the Forestric movement new members had to prove themselves in combat before gaining admittance. At the beginning of the nineteenth century swords were used for the combat; these were later changed for clubs or cudgels, until in 1843 the trial by combat was dropped. As well as testing the mettle of the initiate, this combat was symbolic of Adam's contending with the savage beasts of the field, and the Forester's contending with the world, the flesh and the devil. It may also have functioned as a primitive health check; in the days before formal medical examination became a standard requirement for friendly-society membership, a candidate who could acquit himself creditably in a mock fight was probably reasonably fit to work and support himself. The initiation ceremony also included prayers, an anointing with oil, and a solemn oath to help fellow Foresters and not to reveal Forestric secrets to outsiders.

The RAOF was already unequivocally a benefit society by the early nineteenth century and probably was so from its beginnings. Membership was too expensive for the average industrial worker, and the order probably consisted mostly of skilled artisans and tradesmen.

Discontent grew with the autocratic powers of the officers of the Supreme Court of the Royal Ancient Order of Foresters, and in 1834 a major secession took place at Rochdale; the majority of courts of the order seceded and set up the Ancient Order of Foresters (AOF). The RAOF continued in being and limped on into the 1890s, but in very small numbers; in 1896 it had only twenty-two courts, mostly in south-west Yorkshire, by which time the AOF had nearly five thousand.

In the 1834 reorganisation the AOF introduced a new set of signs and passwords to distinguish itself from the old Royal Order, and a new, slightly revised, ritual was published. It was very biblical in tone – for example, a question on why the bugle horn formed part of the regalia was answered: 'it is considered the most ancient instrument of music ever used, and attached to huntsmen and foresters in all ages. It seems to have been held almost sacred by the Jews, being blown by their High Priests every full moon, and on their

A membership certificate of the Ancient Order of Foresters, dated 1877.

An honorary member's collar of the AOF with pressed base-metal lettering and centre decoration, and gold-bullion fringe and tassels.

Below: *A group of collarettes of the AOF in jacquard-woven silk ribbon.*

solemn feast days, and we read that at the sound of the ram's horns the walls of Jericho fell to the ground.'

The ritual book also contained a form of service for use at a member's funeral or that of a member's wife or widow; the custom of holding funeral ceremonies for members continued into the twentieth century.

The AOF created a rod for its own back at its first High Court Meeting in 1834 by deciding – to prevent the order ever being dominated by a single clique – to have its meetings held in different towns in successive years, with officers appointed from the locality. This meant that a completely inexperienced set of executive officers took post every year and had to learn their jobs from scratch. This proved very unsatisfactory, and eventually this practice had to be dropped and a permanent secretariat appointed. The early records are inconsistent and incomplete, partly for this reason and also because the High Court found it very difficult to get complete and accurate records from subsidiary courts; this tendency continued even

Sash of an officer of a subordinate court of the AOF, with padded satin star and gold-bullion fringe.

Jewel of an officer of a subordinate court of the AOF.

after the new Friendly Societies Act of 1850 enabled the AOF to register for the first time (it had been illegal under the 1793 Rose Act on account of the oath of secrecy).

Nevertheless, the AOF's membership went from strength to strength. In 1845 the order had 1456 courts and 65,909 members. By 1898 it had 4899 courts and 731,442 members and the court funds amounted to £5,119,842. (Not all these new courts were brand-new groups; many were existing village benefit societies that decided to become courts of the AOF.)

Sash of the AOF with monochrome printed silk panel. The pieces of silver braid in the centre are for tying the sash at the hip.

Two sashes of the Ancient Order of Foresters. The one on the left has a padded satin star. That on the right has three padded satin stars, a printed silk panel and gold embroidered lettering.

By the 1860s the AOF's financial state was healthy enough for it to be able to engage in general charity work as well as providing financial support for its members; Foresters regularly raised money for the lifeboat services and the provision of life-saving apparatus on sea coasts, and in 1862 they voted to raise £500 to help depressed textile-manufacturing regions.

Members had to have their characters vouched for and (after 1865) pass a medical examination. Workers in some high-risk occupations were excluded altogether. Sickness, travelling and funeral benefits and benefits for members' widows and orphans were all provided. In the mid nineteenth century most courts met in pubs (it is likely that many pubs called 'The Foresters' Arms' were once the home of an AOF court), and kept their funds in a box with several locks and several key-holders. From 1840 juvenile Forestry courts began to be founded. The main attraction of these was the provision of medical benefits for children.

In the late nineteenth century Forestry spread over the world, particularly to the British colonies but also to the United States. In 1874 a large proportion of the American and Canadian Foresters seceded and set up the Independent Order of Foresters (IOF), which became enormously widespread and prosperous in the United States and Canada. It took on a markedly American flavour, some courts adopting a military-style uniform. The IOF eventually spread back into Britain and gained substantial membership. Jewels of this order are sometimes found in Britain; its emblem is a roundel on a cross with splayed ends and a semicircular curve on the end of each arm; there are little roundels on the ends

118

Two Past Chief Rangers' jewels of the AOF, both in silver, dated 1849 (above left) and 1867 (above right).

Right: *Past Chief Ranger's jewel of the AOF, in base metal.*

Below left: *Treasurer's jewel of the AOF, in silver. The crossed keys are on a background of velvet, now faded and perished.*

Below right: *Pressed base-metal ornament for the centre of a collar of the AOF.*

of the cross arms. In the roundel are a moose's head and the inscription 'I.O.F.'. In the four arms of the cross respectively are a rayed eye, a pair of clasped hands, a robed figure with sword and spear, another robed figure.

In 1883 the American Subsidiary High Court of the AOF passed a law limiting membership to whites in order to expel the Court New Light No. 5667, which had been formed in New Orleans by a group of black men. The High Court of the AOF told them that this was not lawful, citing the General Law of the AOF, which states 'the equal right of all honourable men to become and remain Foresters without reference to creed, colour or country', and the dispute dragged on for years until in 1889 nearly all the remaining American courts declared independence and renamed themselves the Ancient Order of Foresters of America.

In 1892 a proposal was put forward to open the order to women by allowing the formation of female courts. There was some disquiet about this among the membership, not so much because female membership was felt to be inappropriate but on account of fears that women, whose earnings were on average so much lower than those of men, would prove a financial burden on the society. Reassured on this point by the financial buoyancy of the Rechabites, who had had female branches since 1856, and the success of the United Sisters Friendly Society Suffolk Unity, whose president was an

A pre-1892 sash of the AOF, with a printed silk panel showing two male foresters flanking the shield.

A post-1892 honorary member's sash of the AOF, with a printed silk panel showing a male and a female forester flanking the shield.

honorary member of the AOF, the order went ahead with the reform. Indeed, they positively embraced the change by altering the emblem of the order to include the figure of a female forester, and printing separate editions of the ritual and lecture books with the gender appropriately amended.

It must be remembered that all through the nineteenth century there were groups calling themselves 'Foresters' that were not part of the AOF or the IOF. Around 1900 both the Society of Independent Foresters of Clitheroe in Lancashire and the original No. 3 Court of the Royal Foresters at Woolroyd near Leeds, which had operated independently all this time, applied to become courts of the AOF.

Between the wars the AOF was an Approved Society operating within the National Health Insurance Scheme, so it had both voluntary and State members. Unlike many others, it survived the slump in friendly society membership after the creation of the National Health Service in relatively good order, and still flourishes, offering both financial services and social activities just as it did at its inception (although the courts have been renamed 'branches'), as well as supporting a variety of charity work. It also has a lively historical section, which has produced several publications on Forestric history.

EMBLEMS AND SYMBOLS

Early artefacts of the Royal Ancient Order of Foresters tend to include a tailcoated forester shooting a bow, a bugle horn, and a bow and quiver of arrows.

The 1834 membership certificate of the order included God walking in the garden, confronting Adam and Eve in their leaf aprons, and a family scene symbolising unity, benevolence and concord.

Two jewels of the AOF.

In 1835 the AOF emblem was devised. It consists of a shield divided by a cross and has an escutcheon in the centre with bugle horn and bow and arrows. In the top-left quarter of the shield is a pair of clasped hands; in the top-right quarter, three running stags; in the lower-left is a chevron, a lamb and flag above the chevron and a bugle horn below; in the lower-right quarter is a quiver over a bow, arrow and bugle horn. Above the shield is a stag's head issuing out of a coronet; flanking it are the figures of two foresters (both male before 1892, one male and one female thereafter). The motto is 'UNITY, BENEVOLENCE & CONCORD', sometimes given in Latin as 'UNITAS, BENEVOLENTIA, CONCORDIA'.

Apart from the 1892 change, the emblem is consistent in all essentials, but the colours and details such as the foresters' dress can vary widely. Sometimes the All-Seeing Eye surmounts all; often there are extra symbolic decorations (such as rose, thistle and shamrock).

AOF items generally tend to be in an ornate High Victorian decorative style, especially the certificates, which often include vignettes representing charity (the Good Samaritan), unity (a man trying to break a bundle of sticks), obedience (Adam and Eve) and the Peaceable Kingdom (lion, lamb, child).

Where the nature of the artefact does not allow for the whole emblem, the characteristic motifs are a forester; a bow and arrows; a bugle horn; a stag, or a stag's head issuing from a coronet. Oak trees, oak leaves and acorns also tend to feature.

REGALIA AND ARTEFACTS

The form of the personal regalia was laid down in 1834 and included a sash, sometimes known by Foresters as a 'scarf', 6 inches (15.2 cm) wide and 2¼ yards (2.1 metres) long, worn over the right shoulder and tied at the left of the waist. It followed on from a similar form used in the RAOF. The stag's head, the insignia of the order and the initials of the office held were embroidered in gold thread, or shown on an attached panel with the emblem woven or printed in colour or black and white.

Either instead of or as well as the sash was worn a neck-ribbon, 2½ inches (6.3 cm) wide and 1½ yards (1.4 metres) long.

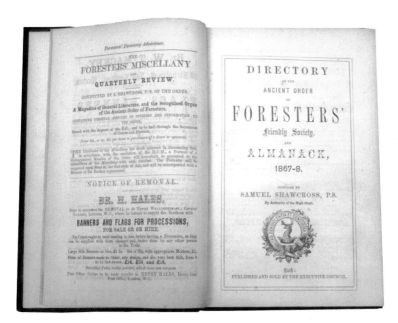

The Directory and Almanack of the AOF, 1867–8.

The colours prescribed in the rulebook of 1898 were as follows. For officers of the High Court the sash was to be green, trimmed at the ends with gold fringe, and the neck-ribbon green with gold stripes at the edges. A Past High Chief Ranger's ribbon was to have a white stripe in the centre. For officers of district courts the sash was to be green, trimmed at the ends with silver fringe, and the neck-ribbon green with white stripes at the edges. A Past District Chief Ranger's ribbon was to have a white stripe in the centre. Officers of subordinate courts were to wear a green sash, trimmed at the ends with scarlet fringe, and a scarlet neck-ribbon with green stripes at the edges. A Past Chief Ranger's ribbon was to have a white stripe in the centre. Members who had not served office were to wear a green sash, trimmed at the ends with green fringe, and a green neck-ribbon. There was a requirement for 'All greens used to be Lincoln green'. All-black sashes and ribbons were prescribed for Forester funeral ceremonies.

By the mid twentieth century a Past Chief Ranger's scarf was red with green edge stripes and a narrow white central stripe – or he or she could use an ordinary scarf with the metal lettering 'P.C.R.' attached to save expense. The neck-ribbon colours were: green and gold for High Court officers; green with pearl-white edge stripes for officers of the district courts; scarlet with green edge stripes for those of the subordinate courts; and plain green for ordinary members. Past Chief Rangers wore a silver medal attached to the ribbon at the centre front. By the 1980s the sash was no longer worn and the neck-ribbon was being worn on its own with a tassel at the centre front (two for Chief Rangers).

Courts were guarded by two Beadles, whose regalia included bugle horns (real cow horns) slung from the left shoulder, and axes. A Senior and Junior Woodward, whose job was to serve all summonses, visit the sick, dispense allowances and take charge of all court property, each carried an axe.

The Ancient Order of Loyal Shepherds

The Ancient Order of Loyal Shepherds was introduced as a second degree of the Ancient Order of Foresters in 1815; thus it was an order within an order, unique among the friendly societies though not uncommon in fraternal ones. It was a way of paying extra contributions and getting extra benefits. In the 1834 reorganisation the order dropped the word 'Loyal' from its title.

Shepherds' meetings were called 'sanctuaries'. A sanctuary and court of the same name and number usually met in the same place but at different times. The two orders usually had the same officers, the chief officer of the Foresters

Membership certificate of the Ancient Order of Shepherds. The emblem of the order is shown in a small shield below the text; the scenes include the Annunciation to the Shepherds (to each side) and the vision of the Peaceable Kingdom described by the Prophet Elijah (at the bottom).

Ornament in pressed base metal for the centre front of a collar. Only the central motif is specific to the Ancient Order of Shepherds; the main body of the item is a standard shape in cheap pressed base metal, punched by the firm of George Tutill, which could be utilised for different societies.

also being the High Pastor of the High Sanctuary. The Shepherds were permitted to form a Supreme Sanctuary in 1826. The Shepherds' order was based on the parable of the Good Shepherd and the 23rd Psalm; their motto was 'THE LORD IS MY SHEPHERD' or, in Latin, 'NOSTER PASTOR EST DOMINUS'. They claimed antiquity from the biblical creation story, calling Abel, the son of Adam, the first shepherd.

Some time between 1880 and 1890 the Ancient Order of Shepherds decided to break the tie and become an independent society.

The emblem of the Ancient Order of Shepherds was a quartered shield: in the top-left quarter was a chain-mail shirt; in the top-right a bow, quiver and arrows; in the lower-left were two crooks, crossed and tied with a ribbon; in the lower-right an almoner's purse. In the centre of the shield was an escutcheon showing a lamb and crook. The motto was 'NOSTER PASTOR EST DOMINUS'.

The Ancient Order of Shepherds was unconnected with the Loyal Order of Ancient Shepherds (Ashton Unity).

Two past officers' jewels of the Ancient Order of Shepherds, 1880s. Both have a suspension bar on the back, so clearly these are breast jewels, intended to hang from a ribbon. The word 'sanctuary' in the inscriptions is the clue that tells us these are AOS jewels.

The Loyal Order of Ancient Shepherds

This order was founded on Christmas Day of 1826 at the Friendship Inn, Old Street, Ashton-under-Lyne, Lancashire, by a group of twelve regulars at that inn, chief among them being the inn's landlord, Thomas Scholfield. These men later became known to the order as the 'Twelve Good Men of Ashton'. They initially sought permission to establish an Oddfellow lodge, but without success, and in the end decided to set up their own order. One of the founder members, a devout Christian recently married to the daughter of a shepherd, suggested that because the society had been founded on Christmas Day and was to help the distressed and show love and brotherhood to all it should be called the 'Ancient Shepherds' in memory of the shepherds in the Christmas story. 'Loyal' was added to dispel any suspicion from the authorities over the objects and activities of the society. The Declaration of the Founders stated that its aim was 'to relieve the sick, bury the dead, and assist each other in all cases of unavoidable distress, so far as in our power lies, and for the promotion of peace and goodwill towards all the human race. In humble imitation of the great Chief Shepherd and SAVIOUR of mankind.'

It further stated that the first lodge was to be called 'The Loyal Abel Lodge No 1' (Abel in the Old Testament story having been a shepherd, as opposed to his brother Cain, who was an arable farmer) and should always meet at the Friendship Inn unless just cause were shown to relocate it; and that no other lodge might be established without the consent of the Loyal Abel Lodge. The head of a lodge was to be called 'Worthy Master'; the president of the order was to be called 'Chief Shepherd'. A Making Ceremony and a Making Song were composed.

The order expanded fast; by the end of 1828 twenty-four more lodges had opened, as far afield as Colne and Wakefield. In 1829 the expansion was such

Transfer-printed jug with the emblem of the Loyal Order of Ancient Shepherds (Ashton Unity).

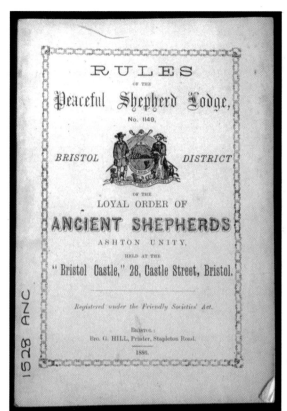

Rulebook of the Peaceful Shepherd Lodge of the Loyal Order of Ancient Shepherds (Ashton Unity), 1886.

that it was necessary to establish separate districts: Ashton, Oldham, Rochdale and Ossett. Such was the importance and respectability of the order that William Gladstone (who from 1865 was Member of Parliament for South Lancashire, the heartland of the Shepherds) became a member. Growth continued throughout the nineteenth century and by the beginning of the First World War the Shepherds had over 143,000 members. Female lodges had been authorised in 1895.

Like the Foresters and Oddfellows, the order became prosperous enough to support charitable causes as well as its own members: in 1876 and again in 1891 it presented a lifeboat, paid for by collections from the members, to the Lifeboat Institution. During the Second World War the Shepherds ran a War Comforts Fund, which funded two motor ambulances and three mobile canteens for the British Red Cross and the Young Men's Christian Association.

The order was still in existence in 2005, now calling itself the Shepherds Friendly Society.

REGALIA AND CEREMONIES

The first public procession of the order was on 31st May (Whit Friday) 1829. From the beginning regalia and ceremonial implements were used in ceremonies and processions: shears (emblematic of sheep-shearing) were to be

Collarette of an honorary member of the Loyal Order of Ancient Shepherds (Ashton Unity), in jacquard-woven silk ribbon.

Collar of a Past Master of the Loyal Order of Ancient Shepherds (Ashton Unity); the metal ornament in the shape of a garter with rose, thistle and shamrock is a standard product from George Tutill, with the order's emblem inserted in the centre.

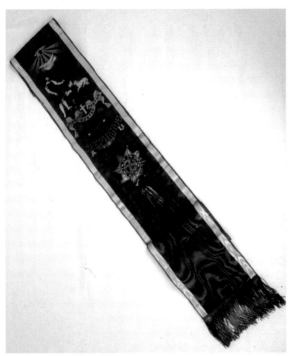

Sash of the Loyal Order of Ancient Shepherds (Ashton Unity), with silver fringe and padded star embroidered in silver thread, with silver-bullion tassel.

carried by the Outside and Inside Guardians, who also wore broad-brimmed hats; members wore lambskin aprons with the wool on; the Past Master wore a crimson ribbon in the fourth buttonhole of the waistcoat and the Chief Shepherd had a mantle. An officer called the 'Minstrel' carried a harp. This title commemorated King David, who according to the Bible had been a shepherd boy and played the harp. It seems that the harp was not a real instrument with strings, as it is described as being 'made of tin' and there is a reference from the 1830s to one being used to make a whip-round: 'That the harp go round the room on behalf of Bro. T. of the Eastern Star Lodge who is suffering under very great affliction and distress' (12s 10d was collected).

The members evidently set great store by their regalia: in October of the fourth year of the society's existence the chief officers felt it necessary to warn against laying 'all their funds out in Pride and Vain bubbles' and 'very expensive Regalia'.

Early Shepherd initiations entailed the candidate being brought in blindfolded while a terrific racket

Past officer's breast jewel of the Loyal Order of Ancient Shepherds (Ashton Unity). The suspended almoner's purse implies that the officer was the lodge almoner.

Jewel of the Loyal Order of Ancient Shepherds (Ashton Unity) in pressed brass, made by George Tutill.

Jewel of the Loyal Order of Ancient Shepherds (Ashton Unity), in base metal. It has a horizontal pin on the back and fastens like a brooch.

was made by the members rattling chairs, shaking sheet-iron to imitate the sound of thunder, clashing swords, stamping their feet and overturning furniture. Then suddenly the noise would stop and the 'beautiful words of the making ceremony' were heard. This practice was toned down, if not abolished, by a resolution of the Annual Moveable Committee in 1835 'to abolish the use of sheet-iron'.

Shepherdry was introduced to Scotland in the 1860s and flourished there. Scottish Shepherds wore their own special processional costume, devised in 1882: a tartan shawl fastened at the left shoulder with a buckle and jewel, a tam-o'-shanter and a long crook. After female lodges were authorised in 1895 Scottish Shepherdesses also wore this costume, with appropriate modifications. It was hugely popular at public events.

The emblem of the Loyal Order of Ancient Shepherds (Ashton Unity) was a shield divided by a St George's cross. In the top-left quarter was a scene of the Adoration of the Shepherds; in the top-right a Calvary cross tilted at an angle; in the lower-left were crossed shepherds' crooks; in the lower-right a crowned man playing a harp (King David). Additional elements varied but might include a beehive, a Latin cross, a lamb, a dove, the motto 'CHRISTUS PASTOR NOSTER', and a shepherd and shepherdess on each side carrying crooks.

The 'Friends'

At least two societies with the word 'Friends' in their title flourished in the nineteenth century and are often confused with each other or assumed to be linked. In fact they do not seem to be connected; but as neither ever registered under friendly-society legislation there is very little concrete information about when they started, when they died out and how widespread they were. What their ritual and 'founding myths' may have been can only be guessed at by study of their artefacts.

THE GRAND ALFRED ORDER OF OLD FRIENDS

The GAOOF flourished in the 1830s and 1840s in London – the *Illustrated London News* published pictures of their processions – and may have been a purely London-based grouping. The order may not have been a benefit society in strict terms but the mottoes on members' aprons, *Nos Fratres Infelices Liberamy* ('we liberate our unhappy brothers') and 'WE RELIEVE A DISTRESS'D BROTHER', place much emphasis on benevolence. It is not known which 'Alfred' their name refers to.

The 1808 issue of an Oddfellows' magazine, the *Thespian Journal*, mentions a body within the Oddfellows called the 'Grand Alfred Independent Order', described as 'A Fund for the Relief of distressed Brothers, and their Widows and Orphans ... established July 15, 1807', with four lodges. It is possible that the GAOOF of the later nineteenth century is the descendant of this body, having split off from the Oddfellows and begun to operate independently. The emphasis on 'relief of distressed brothers' would seem to back up this speculation; on the other hand, the iconography of their artefacts bears no clear resemblance to Oddfellows symbolism. More research is needed to find this order's place within friendly-society history.

Below: *Jewel of the GAOOF, with fixing lugs. The caption says 'A MARK OF RESPECT TO AN IMPROVED P.N.O.F.' (which possibly stands for Past Noble Old Friend).*

Above left: *Jewel of the GAOOF. It has three fixing lugs on the reverse and may have been intended to be stitched to the centre front of a collar.*

Engraved glass panel with the symbols of the GAOOF.

Brass figurine of a man dressed in the style of the 1820s and 1830s, wearing an apron with the symbols of the GAOOF. There are holes in the feet, presumably to peg the figurine to a larger item.

Pewter snuffbox with the symbols of the GAOOF.

At least four variants of the GAOOF emblem can be identified. These are described below.

Variant 1: an assemblage with, at the top, a rayed eye, then stars or flowers, a cross, a pair of crossed swords, crossed keys, a four-runged ladder, a set square, a crown above two horizontal swords, the letters 'G A O O F', and the motto 'WE RELIEVE A DISTRESS'D BROTHER'.

Variant 2: numbered panels in each corner depict (top left) a seated bearded king, holding a book and sword, next to a pillar, numbered 1; (top right) Hope holding her anchor, numbered 2; (bottom left) a female figure (possibly Fame?) holding some writing and blowing a trumpet, numbered 3; (bottom right) a trophy of flags (including a Union flag), an anchor and a cannon. At

Painted composition snuffbox with the emblem of the Grand Alfred Order of Old Friends variant 1.

Below: *Spectacle case with the emblem of the GAOOF variant 1.*

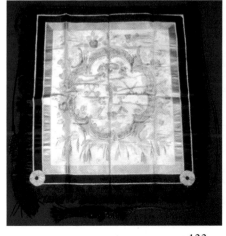

Hand-painted apron of the GAOOF with emblem variant 1.

Painted tin box with the emblem of the GAOOF variant 1.

the top is the rayed eye over a crown and two horizontal swords pointing outwards, surrounded by the letters 'G A O O F'. In the centre is a man wearing early-nineteenth-century dress and a collarette with pendant jewels, holding a book entitled *Charitable Purposes* and sitting at a desk on which is a paper headed 'LAWS of the lodge', under a draped canopy with the words '*Nos Fratres Infelices Liberamy*', flanked by (usually) two extra letters. On the left are a key and sword with guard, a jewel with a monogram on a ribbon, and a four-runged ladder; on the right are a sword with guard and set square, a jewel with a monogram on a ribbon, and crossed quills. Below the seated figure is a scroll with the words '*GLORY be to GOD above*', below this crossed keys, and below this a scene of square-rigged ships on the sea.

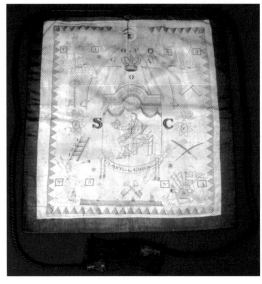

Printed silk apron of the GAOOF with emblem variant 2.

Two printed silk aprons of the GAOOF with emblem variant 3.

Variant 3: numbered panels in each corner depict (top left) a seated bearded king, holding a book and sword, next to a pillar, numbered 1; (top right) Hope holding her anchor, numbered 2; (bottom left) a female figure (possibly Fame?) holding some writing and blowing a trumpet, numbered 3; (bottom right) a trophy of flags (including a Union flag), an anchor and a cannon. At the top the rayed eye is over a cross; below this are a crown and two horizontal swords pointing outwards, surrounded by the letters 'G A O O F G F', with scrolls reading 'GLORY BE TO GOD ABOVE' and 'FRATRI LABORANTIBUS SUCCURRIMUBUS'. Flanking this on the left are crossed keys above a four-runged ladder, on the right crossed swords, a set square and an upright sword. Below this is a scene of square-rigged ships on the sea.

Printed silk apron of the GAOOF with emblem variant 4.

Variant 4: numbered panels in each corner depicting (top left) a seated bearded king, holding a book and sword, next to a pillar, numbered 1; (top right) Hope holding her anchor, numbered 2; (bottom left) a female figure (possibly Fame?) holding some writing and blowing a trumpet, numbered 3; (bottom right) a trophy of flags (including a Union flag), an anchor and a cannon. At the top the rayed eye is over a cross; below this are a crown and two horizontal swords pointing inwards, surrounded by the letters 'G A O O F G F', with scrolls reading 'GLORY BE TO GOD ABOVE' and 'WE ASSIST OUR BRETHREN IN TIME OF NEED'. Flanking this on the left are crossed keys above a four-runged ladder and an upright sword, on the right crossed swords, a set square and an upright sword. Below this is a scene of square-rigged ships on the sea.

LOYAL UNITED FRIENDS

This society was founded in London, at 19 Princelet Street, Spitalfields. The building still survives and is preserved as the Spitalfields Centre; it is open to the public on selected days. According to the research of the Spitalfields Centre, the Loyal United Friends were formed by a group of Jewish immigrants, mostly from Poland. Like the GAOOF, they may always have been local to London, where they seem to have flourished between the 1850s and 1890s; they had at least fifty-three lodges.

If the founders of the Loyal United Friends were indeed Polish Jews, the iconography of their artefacts is remarkable for its Englishness; each individual symbol is typical of the English friendly-society tradition, as is the general

19 Princelet Street, Spitalfields, the original headquarters of the Loyal United Friends.

Hand-painted apron of the Loyal United Friends.

Silk-printed apron of the Loyal United Friends.

Silk-printed apron of the Loyal United Friends – a different print from that in the previous illustration. The knot of ribbons stitched at the centre top is a relic of the old way of fastening the waist-ties at the front.

Sash of the Loyal United Friends. The black velvet panel may denote a mourning sash, or it may originally have had a printed silk panel stitched over it.

layout and style. Certainly the membership of the society must have become more general very quickly, as all the named artefacts the author has seen have traditional English names: 'Waghorn', 'Cooper', 'Lockyer', 'Clements', 'Hall', 'Anstey'.

The Loyal United Friends' emblem depicts a temple on a chequered carpet with a figure of Charity (a woman with children) in the doorway and the Dove of the Holy Spirit descending in the pediment, between two pillars, the left-hand pillar bearing the letter 'C' (*Caelum*?) on the base and with a celestial globe on top, the right-hand pillar bearing the letter 'T' (*Terra*?) on the base and with a terrestrial globe on top. Between the pillars are a four-runged ladder (the rungs sometimes being labelled with the four cardinal virtues), a raised hand, a crown, an open Bible, a rose on a branch, a rayed sun surrounded by the letters 'T E V R P M D N I M E H' (the meaning of these letters is obscure), the moon and seven stars, all below the rayed eye.

Silver suspension bar from a breast jewel of the Loyal United Friends.

139

Six silver breast jewels of the Loyal United Friends, in a variety of characteristic shapes, some with the emblem of the order in the centre.

Above: *Painted wooden snuffbox with the emblem of the Loyal United Friends – a very similar box to that of the GAOOF illustrated on page 133.*

Left: *Ceremonial mace or sceptre of the Loyal United Friends.*

On certificates and aprons the emblem is often surrounded by cartouches at the corners containing figures of the cardinal virtues, sprays of fruiting oak and laurel at the sides and bottom, and a scroll over the top edge reading 'LOYAL UNITED FRIENDS'.

Painted tin box with the emblem of the Loyal United Friends; a very similar GAOOF box is illustrated on page 134.

The temperance orders

It was not only the authorities who objected to the link between the friendly societies and the pub. Drunkenness was a real social problem in nineteenth-century Britain, and reformers from a great variety of political and religious backgrounds campaigned for temperance. (Early reformers distinguished between 'abstinence' from alcohol and 'temperance' in its old meaning of 'moderation', but increasingly the two words were used as synonyms.) Campaigners for temperance deplored the association of mutual self-help with social drinking; the logical solution was to form temperance friendly societies, which would not only include no alcohol in their social meetings but would positively promote the campaign against drink.

The temperance friendly societies were very successful. In the mid nineteenth century, when habitual drunkenness was a national scandal, teetotallers were likely to be healthier and more financially prudent and have fewer accidents than the average of the population, and this benefited the finances of the temperance societies. In the second half of the twentieth century the common ethos and social purpose of the temperance societies helped them keep their membership when other societies melted away after the introduction of universal state provision.

THE RECHABITES

The earliest of the important temperance friendly societies was founded in

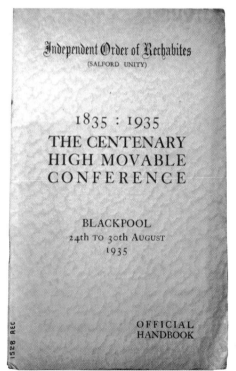

Handbook of the Centenary Conference of the Rechabite order, 1935.

Two Rechabite lapel badges.

Lancashire by the 'Seven Men of Preston', who put their names to a pledge to abstain totally from all intoxicating liquors in August 1833. The man who drew up the pledge, Joseph Livesey, published a newspaper, the *Preston Temperance Advocate*. In July 1835 a reader suggested the formation of a teetotal order, along the lines of the Oddfellows; a Temperance Burial Society already existed around that time in nearby Salford, meeting at the Salford Temperance Coffee House, with the modest objective of helping to defray the funeral expenses of members. Livesey took up the suggestion in his editorial columns and very soon the new order came into being in Salford – effectively a re-launch of the earlier society.

The founders chose to name their order after the sons of Rechab, whose story is told in chapter 35 of the Book of Jeremiah in the Old Testament:

> And I set before the sons of the house of the Rechabites pots full of wine, and cups, and I said unto them, Drink ye wine. But they said, We will drink no wine: for Jonadab the son of Rechab our father commanded us saying, Ye shall drink no wine, neither ye, nor your sons for ever. Neither shall ye build house, nor sow seed, nor plant vineyard, nor have any: but all your days ye shall dwell in tents; that ye may live many days in the land where ye be strangers.

The organisational structure of the order was drawn directly from existing models such as Oddfellowship and Masonry, but the imagery drew heavily on the story of the Rechabites and the Bible in general. The lodges were known as 'tents', since the biblical Rechabites had 'dwelt in tents', the first being Tent Ebenezer No. 1, opened on 25th August 1835. The head of each tent was the High Chief Ruler, assisted by officers with titles such as 'Guardian' and 'Levite'.

The emblem took the form of a rather crowded heraldic-style shield containing among other things three wigwam-shaped tents on a

Jewel of a Past Chief Ruler of the Rechabites (with the monogram 'PCR' in the centre), in silver and enamel.

143

Above: *Silver and silver-gilt jewel of the Rechabites, probably for fixing to the centre front of a collar, with the emblem of the order in the centre.*

Right: *Rechabite breast jewel in bronze, illustrating the biblical story of the sons of Rechab, with the motto 'WE WILL DRINK NO WINE'.*

chevron, a serpent and two doves representing Christ's injunction in Matthew, chapter 10 verse 16, 'Be ye therefore wise as serpents, and harmless as doves', and the sun and the moon with stars – probably influenced by mainstream fraternal/friendly-society symbolism. Two maidens flanked the shield, bearing a palm (symbolising peace) and a cornucopia (for plenty). Above the shield were a beehive, wheat

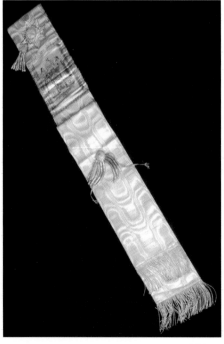

Rechabite sash, in silk with silver fringe, tassels and embroidery and silk-printed panel with the emblem of the order.

Rechabite apron, in silk with silver fringe, tassels and embroidery and silk-printed panel with the emblem of the order.

sheaves and a crossed palm branch and sword. The motto was 'PEACE AND PLENTY THE REWARD OF TEMPERANCE'. Sometimes there is a scene of the biblical Rechabites refusing wine, often with the phrase 'WE WILL DRINK NO WINE'.

With the initial assistance of publicity from the *Preston Temperance Advocate*, the new movement spread fast. A second Salford tent was established in November 1835, and the order spread out through Lancashire. By 1836 it had reached the Isle of Man, and by 1838 the first tent was established in Scotland. Although not a sectarian movement, it was strongly associated with the Primitive Methodists, which no doubt helped it spread. Female tents and juvenile tents (for children as young as five) were not slow to appear.

In 2005 the Rechabites were based in Manchester, very close to their place of origin, and continue their social temperance activity. However, their financial services arm, Healthy Investment Limited, bowed to market forces in July 2003 and for the first time made its savings and insurance plans available to non-teetotallers.

THE TOTAL ABSTINENT SONS AND SISTERS OF THE PHOENIX

The Sons and Sisters of the Phoenix were a little-known but evidently very vigorous temperance group that flourished mainly in London and the south-east of England from the 1870s onwards. There were at least two main orders – the Original Grand Order of the Total Abstinent Sons of the Phoenix (OGOTASP) and the United Order of the Total Abstinent Sons of the Phoenix (UOTASP). They may have merged at some point, as artefacts exist with the initials 'U&OGOTASP'. Another group, with the initials 'IJGOTASP', has not been identified.

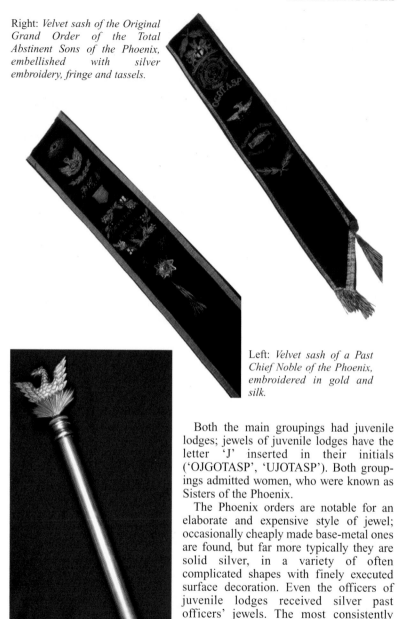

Right: *Velvet sash of the Original Grand Order of the Total Abstinent Sons of the Phoenix, embellished with silver embroidery, fringe and tassels.*

Left: *Velvet sash of a Past Chief Noble of the Phoenix, embroidered in gold and silk.*

Both the main groupings had juvenile lodges; jewels of juvenile lodges have the letter 'J' inserted in their initials ('OJGOTASP', 'UJOTASP'). Both group-ings admitted women, who were known as Sisters of the Phoenix.

The Phoenix orders are notable for an elaborate and expensive style of jewel; occasionally cheaply made base-metal ones are found, but far more typically they are solid silver, in a variety of often complicated shapes with finely executed surface decoration. Even the officers of juvenile lodges received silver past officers' jewels. The most consistently appearing motif is the phoenix rising from the flames, which is a symbol of rebirth and resurrection; often this is the only symbol shown, but sometimes there is a whole

Sceptre of an officer of the Phoenix.

A silver presentation jewel of a Past Chief Noble of the OGOTASP, with, on the obverse (above left), a portrait photograph of the recipient in his regalia and holding a sceptre, and on the reverse (above right) a presentation inscription: 1870.

group of esoteric symbols – a globe, figures of Mercury and Death, an owl, a book – which suggests that the Sons of the Phoenix may have had an elaborate ritual system.

The head of a male Phoenix lodge had the title Chief Noble; the letters 'PCN' (Past Chief Noble) frequently appear on jewels and sashes. The female equivalent had the initials 'PCM' – possibly standing for Past Chief Matron, but this is not certain.

Typically breast jewels of the OGOTASP have red and white ribbons, and the UOTASP blue and white, but this is not consistent.

Far left: *Jewel of a Past Chief Noble of the Limehouse Lifeboat Lodge of the OGOTASP, 1886. The central roundel is of gilt and red foil under a watch-glass.*

Near left: *Jewel of a Past Chief Noble of the OGOTASP, 1884.*

147

Top left: *Jewel of the Assistant Secretary of a Phoenix order, probably the OJGOTASP, 1884.*

Top right: *Jewel of a Past Chief Noble of the OJGOTASP, 1883.*

Left: *Jewel of a Past Chief Noble of the OGOTASP, with symbols including Death and Mercury in the central roundel.*

Bottom left: *Jewel of a Past Chief Noble of a Phoenix order, probably the UJOTASP, 1890.*

Bottom centre: *Jewel of a Past Chief Noble of the UOTASP.*

Bottom right: *Jewel of a Past Chief Noble of the OGOTASP, 1883.*

Above left: *Jewel of a Past Chief Noble of the OJGOTASP, 1883.*

Above right: *Jewel of a Past Chief Noble of the OJGOTASP, 1894.*

THE SONS OF TEMPERANCE

The Order of the Sons of Temperance was formed in New York in September 1842. It was a friendly society that aimed to provide sickness and death benefits, but also to shield its members from the evils of intemperance, to campaign against drunkenness, and to assist in every way the suppression of the alcohol trade. Members pledged at their initiation: 'I will neither make, buy, sell nor use as a beverage, any spiritous or malt liquors, wine or cider.' The order spread rapidly and had eminent supporters; three presidents of the United States – Abraham Lincoln, Rutherford B. Hayes and Ulysses S. Grant – were members of the Sons of Temperance.

The order was introduced into the United Kingdom in 1849, the first division being formed in a rough district of Liverpool, and by 1855 it was widespread enough that a

Collar of the Sons of Temperance, in cloth with ribbon binding and rosette.

National Division of Great Britain and Ireland was organised on 6th April 1855 by permission of the North American National Division.

Juvenile members of the order were called Cadets of Temperance; the Cadets were first introduced in Liverpool as early as 1850. In 1889 the National Division Executive appointed a Most Worthy Patron to be responsible for the oversight of working Sections in conjunction with the Band of Hope, and to promote the welfare of the Cadets in citizenship and temperance education through meetings, competitions and other activities.

In 2005 the order still existed in Britain, as the Sons of Temperance Friendly Society, and continued to restrict its financial services to teetotallers.

THE INDEPENDENT ORDER OF GOOD TEMPLARS

The Independent Order of Good Templars was founded in Utica, New York, in 1851, with the objective of uniting all temperance organisations; unlike the Rechabites and the Phoenix, it had no mutual benefit aspect but aimed solely to campaign against alcohol. Its ritual structure was ultimately derived from Freemasonry (it has been described as 'Teetotal Freemasonry'), with a system of three degrees: the first or Initiatory degree; the second, or degree of Fidelity; and the third, or degree of Charity. There was also an inner circle of senior members belonging to the Council degree. Every initiate had to make a lifelong pledge to abstain from using, or giving or selling to others, 'anything that will intoxicate'.

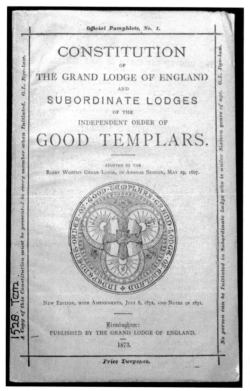

Constitution of the Grand Lodge of England of the Independent Order of Good Templars.

Sash of the Independent Order of Good Templars, in jacquard-woven silk ribbon.

The order was named after the medieval Knights Templar, and accordingly the lodges of the higher degrees were known as 'temples', officers had titles such as Commander, Guard, Sentinel and Marshal, and members were to see themselves as valiant knights fighting a crusade against drink. However, the Good Templars also used other moral imagery, such as the story of the Old

Commemorative medal of the Independent Order of Good Templars United Temperance Fête, obverse (above left) and reverse (above right).

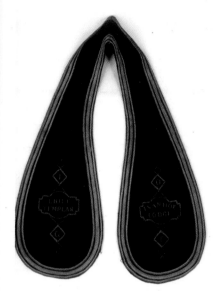

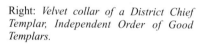

Velvet collar of a Chief Templar, Independent Order of Good Templars.

Right: *Velvet collar of a District Chief Templar, Independent Order of Good Templars.*

Velvet collar of the Independent Order of Good Templars. The symbols of Faith, Hope and Charity are embroidered in gold on each breast and a commemorative medal is pinned on.

Secretary's jewel of the Independent Order of Good Templars Grand Lodge of India, inscribed 'Afghanistan 1878–9–80'; presumably the owner was based in the Indian Army.

Testament Rechabites, and braced its members with songs to well-known patriotic tunes:

> We are gathering for the conflict with earnest
> hearts and true,
> Shouting the battle cry of temperance,
> The world will bless our progress in the work we
> have to do;
> Cold water forever, hurrah! then, hurrah!
> Down with the wine glass – up with our star;
> As we gather for a right cause, with earnest
> hearts and true,
> Shouting the battle cry of temperance.

The most striking innovation of the Good Templars was its membership. Not only did it admit whites and blacks on terms of perfect equality – otherwise unheard of in the United States at that time – but it was the first temperance order to admit women alongside men in mixed-sex lodges.

The first Good Templar lodge in Britain opened in 1868 in Birmingham, and the order spread rapidly; by 1871 there were three hundred British lodges, with over twenty thousand members. Juvenile Templary began in the United States in 1868 and spread to England in the early 1870s. Children could be enrolled

Group photograph of a lodge of Good Templars, 1927.

as Infant Templars from birth, Juvenile Templars from the age of five, and could join a senior temple at twelve.

As the order spread worldwide it changed its name to 'International Order of Good Templars', and finally to 'International Organisation of Good Templars'. It became a very influential body (it was among the pressure groups that lobbied for Prohibition in the United States) and in 2005 was still very widespread throughout the world, with its headquarters in Sweden.

The emblem of the Independent Order of Good Templars was a shield bearing a cross with splayed ends, and a central escutcheon with three standing lions vertically above one another.

Postscript

Many friendly and fraternal societies must have existed in the eighteenth and nineteenth centuries – small fraternal groups and unregistered friendly societies – whose names and existence are now wholly lost. Conversely, there are many whose existence is recorded, in local government archives and the Friendly Societies Register, but of whose myths, character and regalia nothing is known.

Thus, in any mixed group of friendly and fraternal regalia there are likely to be items that it is impossible to identify with any specific society. Some of these are unidentifiable because they are unremarkable and, lacking an inscription, might belong to any number of societies; others, despite being distinctive, are wholly mysterious. More research in the field will no doubt identify many of these, but it may be that only sheer chance will help us put a name to others.

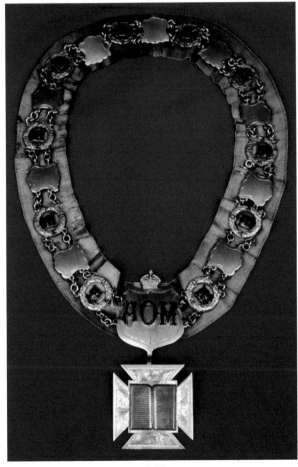

Chain-collar of an unknown society.

Further reading

Buckley, Anthony D., and Anderson, T. Kenneth. *Brotherhoods in Ireland.* Ulster Folk Museum, 1988. A brief illustrated guide to the very different fraternities of Ireland.

Cooper, Walter G. *The Ancient Order of Foresters Friendly Society: 150 Years 1834–1984.* Ancient Order of Foresters Friendly Society, 1984.

Cordery, Simon. *British Friendly Societies 1759–1914.* Palgrave Macmillan, 2003.

Fisk, Audrey, and Logan, Roger. *Grandfather Was in the Foresters.* Ancient Order of Foresters Friendly Society, 1994.

Fowler, Simon. *Sources for Labour History.* Public Record Office, 1995.

Gosden, P. H. J. H. *The Friendly Societies in England, 1815–1875.* Manchester University Press, 1961.

Jackson, Keith B. *Beyond the Craft.* Addlestone, 1994. An illustrated guide to the 'side orders' of Freemasonry, and their regalia.

Logan, Roger. *An Introduction to Friendly Society Records.* Federation of Family History Societies, 2000.

Collarette of the same unknown society as the chain collar on the previous page. It has been suggested that the letters 'AOM' on these charming artefacts stand for 'Ancient Order of Mousers', but nobody knows for sure.

Research resources

The Ancient Order of Foresters Heritage Trust, 12–13 College Place, Southampton SO15 2FE. Website: www.foresters.ws (The AOF has archives and an active historical unit.)

The Association of Friendly Societies, 10–13 Lovat Lane, London EC3R 8DT. Telephone: 020 7397 9550. Website: www.afs.org.uk (This body co-ordinates and represents the friendly societies still offering financial services in the United Kingdom; its website lists these with contact details.)

The Friendly Societies Research Group, Faculty of Social Sciences, Open University, Walton Hall, Milton Keynes MK7 6AA. Website: www.open.ac.uk/socialsciences/fsrg

The Grand United Order of the Knights of the Golden Horn. Website: www.guokgh.org.uk

The National Archives (previously the Public Records Office), Kew, Richmond, Surrey TW9 4DU. Website: www.nationalarchives.gov.uk (Historical records of all registered friendly societies are to be found here in the FS group.)

The Self-help in Edinburgh, Lothians and Fife Digitisation Project. Website: www.historyshelf/org (An interesting site focusing on societies in eastern Scotland.)

University of Hull Brynmor Jones Library (Archives and Special Collections), Cottingham Road, Kingston upon Hull HU6 7RX. Telephone: 01482 465265. Website: www.hull.ac.uk/arc

Places to visit

The John Goodchild Collection, below Central Library, Drury Lane, Wakefield WF1 2DT. Telephone: 01924 298929. (A very large collection of friendly society documents and artefacts of all kinds; privately owned but open to the public by appointment.)

The Library and Museum of Freemasonry, Freemasons' Hall, 60 Great Queen Street, London WC2B 5AZ. Telephone: 020 7395 9257. Website: www.freemasonry.london.museum (In addition to its core Masonic collections, it has large holdings of non-Masonic fraternal and friendly society material that are not normally on display.)

Museum of English Rural Life, The University of Reading, PO Box 229, Whiteknights, Reading RG6 6AG. Telephone: 0118 378 8660. Website: www.ruralhistory.org (Particularly notable for its collection of metal pole-heads from friendly society banners and processional staffs.)

The People's History Museum, The Pump House, Bridge Street, Manchester M3 3ER. Telephone: 0161 839 6061. Website: www.peopleshistorymuseum.org.uk (Has large collections of friendly society and trade union material, including a particularly fine collection of banners.)

Royal Antediluvian Order of Buffaloes Grand Lodge of England Museum, Grove House, Skipton Road, Harrogate, North Yorkshire HG1 4LA. Telephone: 01423 502438. Website: www.raobgle.org.uk (Has holdings of Knights of the Golden Horn regalia as well as RAOB material.)

The Spitalfields Centre, 19 Princelet Street, London E1 6QH. Telephone: 020 7247 5352. Website: www.19princeletstreet.org.uk (Open only a few days a year because of the fragile state of the building.)

Index

Page references in italic relate to illustrations or their captions.

Acorns: **see** Oak
Adam and Eve, as symbol 52, *84*, 85, 114, 121-2
Affiliated orders 18, 23
Almoner's purse, as symbol 50, *129*
America, United States of, friendly and fraternal activity in 19, 21, 92, 103, 118-20, 149, 150, 153
Anatomy Act (1822) 15
Anchor, as symbol of hope 52, 135; **see also** Virtues
Ancient Order of Foresters: **see** Foresters
Ancient Order of Shepherds: **see** Shepherds
Aprons 31-4, 74 , 92, 96, 110, 129
Ashmole, Elias 57
Australia, friendly and fraternal activity in 84, 95, 103
Axes 123
Banners 16, 31, 47
Bees and beehive, as symbols 53, 97, *129*, 130, 144
Bevin reforms 27, 84
Book, as symbol *18*, 51
Bow and arrows, as symbols 121, 122, 125
Boxes, including snuffboxes, matchboxes 34, *43*, *132*, *141*
British Empire 19
Bromley, Kent 50
Buck, as symbol: **see** Stag
Bucks, Most Ancient and Honourable Society of 6-9, *7*, *8*, 101
Buffaloes, Royal Antediluvian Order of 13, *32*, *40*, 70-6, *70*, *71*, *75*, 77; Banners *75*, 76; Certified Primo Degree 72; Glades (women's lodges) 76; Kangaroo Degree 70, *72*; Knight Order of Merit Degree *72*, 74; museum 79; Roll of Honour Degree *73*, 74
Bugle horn: **see** Horn, hunting
Burial: **see** Funerals

Cadets of Temperance: **see** Sons of Temperance
Canada, friendly and fraternal activity in *19*, 118-20
Carpet, in lodge furnishing and as symbol 55, 60, *60*, 139
Cat, as symbol *155-6*
Ceramics 43, *43*, *81*, *99*, 100, *100*, 111, *126*
Certificates of membership 45, *47*, 76, 82, *109*, 115, *124*
Charity: **see** Virtues
Chartism 13
Church, attitude to rituals 18-19
Churchill, Winston, member of AOD 110
Clocks 43, *44*
Coffin, as symbol: **see** Mortality, emblem of
Collars and collarettes 34-6, 60, 110, 122
Combination Acts 14
Commandments, Ten, as symbol 53
Commemorative jewels and medals 40, *63*
Constantinople 79
Cornucopia, as symbol 51, 107, 144
Craft lodge tradition 6
Crooks, shepherds', used in lodges and as symbol 43, 108, *110*, *111*, 113, *129*, 130
Cross, as symbol 53, 130, 133-6, 154
Crown, as symbol 54, 134-6, 139
Cumberland, Duke of 17
David, King, as shepherd 129
Death, as symbol: **see** Mortality, emblem of
Defoe, Daniel 4
Dove, as symbol 52, 53, 97, 130, 139, 144
Druids, orders of 43, *46*, 56, 101-13; Ancient Order of *18*, 40, *47*, *50*, 51, 103, 105-7, *106*, *107*, 110, *110*, *112*; Council of British Druid Orders 106-7; Druidical

Congresses *109*; Druids Sheffield Friendly Society 109; Grand Independent Lodge of Ancient 51; Grand Lodge of *112*; Order of 107-8, *108*, *109*; Royal Arch Chapter of the AOD 105, *107*, *112*; Sheffield Independent Druids 109; United Ancient Order of 21, 103-5, *104*, *105*
Eye, as symbol *30*, 53, 97, 122, 133-6, 139
Faith: **see** Virtues
Fasces, Fascism, Fascists 53, 67, 107
Feasts 4, 15-16, 22, 23-5
First World War 84
Flat-iron stands 43, *44*
Foresters, Ancient Order of 17, 19, 23-5, 27, 28, *29*, *31*, *32*, *37*, *38*, *41*, 42, *45*, 49, 51, 114-23, *115*, *116*, *117*, *118*, *119*, *121*; admit women (1892) 120-1; Foresters' Almanack *123*; Foresters, Independent Order of (USA and Canada) 19-21, *20*, 118-20; *Foresters' Miscellany* 23-5, *24*, 45; Foresters of America, Ancient Order of 120; Independent Foresters of Clitheroe 121; juvenile lodges 118; Royal Ancient Order of 114-15
Fortitude: **see** Virtues
Fox, Charles James 9
Free Gardeners, orders of 5, 34, *43*, *45*, 81-9, *81*, *82*, *83*, *84*, *85*, *86*, *87*, *88*, *89*; Ancient Order of *33*, 81-9; British Order of Free Gardeners 84; Fraternitie of the Gairdners of East Lothian 81-4; Gardeners Preservation Society 84; Loyal and Independent Gardeners 89; National United Order of Free Gardeners Friendly Society 81; Order of Ancient 81; Order of Ancient Free Gardeners

Lancashire Union 83; Order of Free Gardeners 84; ritual of 84-6; St Andrews Order of *45*, 81; St John's Lodge of *5*; symbolism of 54, 85-9

Freemasons 5, 7, 11, *43, 44*, 49, 51, 57-69, *57, 58, 60, 61, 62*, 101; Allied Masonic Degrees 65; Ancient and Accepted Rite ('Scots Rite') 64, *66*; Antients and Moderns 58, *58*, 59, 62; Co-Masonry *68*, 69; craft degrees 57, 59, *59*; female freemasonry 68-9; Freemasons' Hall 60; Grand Lodge of Ireland, 68-9, *69*; Grand Lodge of Scotland 68-9, *69*; Honourable Order of Ancient Freemasons 69; Knights of Malta 62-4; Mark Masonry 62, *63*; Masonic Knights Templar 58, 62-4, *64*, 79; Operative Masons 65; Order of the Secret Monitor 64, *65*; Order of Women Masons 69; Royal and Select Masters 62, *63*; Royal Arch Degree 58, *58*; Royal Ark Mariners 62, *63*; Royal Masonic Benevolent Institution 60; Royal Masonic Hospital 60; Royal Masonic Institution for Boys 60; Royal Masonic Institution for Girls 60; Royal Order of Scotland 65; Scottish Freemasons 34; side degrees 62-5, *66*; symbolism of 53; United Grand Lodge of England 58, 62

French Revolution 9

Friendly Brothers of St Patrick: **see** St Patrick, Friendly Brothers of

Friendly Societies legislation 4, 13, 15, 16, 117

Friends, orders of 131-41; Grand Alfred Order of Old Friends 131-6, *131-6*; Loyal United Friends 136-41; *137-41*; Ye Olde Friends *45*

Frothblowers, Ancient Order of 26, *26*

Funerals, funeral benefits, funeral regalia 4, 5, 18-19, 41-2, *41, 42, 95,* 116

Furniture for lodges 42-3, 60

Gardeners: **see** Free Gardeners

Gauntlets 36-7, *36, 59, 73*, 74

George Tutill 29, *29, 108, 125, 128, 130*

Gladstone, W. E., member of LOAS 127

Globe, as symbol 54, 96, 139, 147

Golden Horn, Knights of *36*, 77-80, *77, 78, 79*; Grand United Order of the 79; Novocastria Encampment *79*; Order of the Shield *78*

Golden Section, as symbol 54, *61, 68*

Good Templars, Independent Order of 21 150-4; *151, 152, 153*; Juvenile Templars 153-4

Goose and Gridiron tavern 57

Great Exhibition of 1851 23, *24*

Gregorians, Society of 9, *10, 11*, 11, 90

Groves (UAOD lodges) 103

Guilds 4, 5, 82

Hand, as symbol *27, 45, 100, 129*, 139; heart on hand 96, *99*

Harp, as symbol 51, 129; **see also** Lyre

Harp Tavern 70

Heart, as symbol of Charity 52; **see also** Hand

Henry Slingsby 29

Honorary members of societies 40

Hope: **see** Virtues

Horn, hunting, as symbol 80, *80*, 115, 121, 122, 123

Horse, as symbol of Kent *50, 56*

Huguenots 5

Hurle, Druid founder 101-2, 111

Incorporations 82-3

Initiation and initiation ceremonies 6, 15, 91-2, 114, 129-30

Ireland, friendly and fraternal activity in 12, 16, 68-9

Jerusalem Sols, Royal Grand Order of 6, *7*

Jewels 38-40

Jews and Jewish friendly societies 6, *20*, 21, 82, 90, 136-7, 115

Justice: **see** Virtues

Juvenile lodges and societies 22, *23*, 118, 146, 149, *149,* 153

Kenning, George, manufacturer 29

Key, as symbol *8,* 51, 97, 98, *119,* 133

King's Arms, Soho 101

Knights of the Golden Horn: **see** Golden Horn, Knights of

Knights Templar (Masonic): **see** Freemasonry

Ladder, as symbol 52, 133-6, 139; **see also** Virtues

Lamb, lamb and flag, lamb and cross, as symbols 53, 97, 125, *129*, 130

Lion, as symbol 154

Lloyd George, David 4, 26

London Corresponding Society 9

Loyal Britons, Lodge of *12*

Loyal Order of Ancient Shepherds (Ashton Unity) **see** Shepherds

Lushington, City of (stage guild) 70

Lyre, as symbol 51, *103*; **see also** Harp

Maccabeans, Order of Ancient *20*

Maces: **see** Sceptres and maces

Man, Isle of 16, 22

Manx Liberal (newspaper) 22

Markfield Female Friendly Society 22

Mask, as symbol and in ritual 55, 92, *99*

Mercury as symbol *39,* 147

Mortality, emblem of 14, *39, 42,* 53-4, 92, 97, 147

Mourning: **see** Funerals

Mussolini, Benito 53

National Conference of Friendly Societies *26*

National Insurance 4, 26, 27, 84, 95, 121

Nelson, Admiral Horatio *8*

Nimrod 6-7

Noah and Noah's Ark, as symbol 52, 85, *85, 87, 88,* 97

Oak and acorns, as symbol 43, 55, *104,* 108, *109, 110,* 113, 122

Oddfellows 18, 28, 42, *42, 44, 46, 47,* 49, 90-100, *91, 99,* 126, 131; Albion Order of 93; Ancient Noble Order of (Bolton Unity) 93; British United Order of 93; Caledonian Order of *96,* 97; *Complete Manual of Oddfellowship 47,* 90, 92-4; costumes and rank, titles of 90; Grand Lodge of Kent Independent Order of (Kent Unity) *41,* 94, *95,* 97; Grand United Order of 92, 93, 95; Improved Independent Order of 93; in North America 92, *100;* initiation ritual of 91-2; Kingston Unity of 94, 95; Loyal Aristarcus Lodge 90, *94;* Manchester Unity 15, *35, 39, 40,* 42, *43, 46,* 92, 93, *93, 94,* 95, 97, *98, 99, 100;* National Independent Order of 94, 95; Nottingham Imperial Order of *36,* 51, 90, 93, 99-100; Patriotic or Union Order 90-2; regalia and symbolism of 95-100; symbolism of 53, 56; Wolverhampton Unity of 94; women in 95

Orange Order 16-17, *17, 30, 33, 35*

Owl, as symbol 147

Palm, as symbol 54, 144-5

Paul, St 51

Peaceable Kingdom, as symbol 52, *124*

Phoenix, as symbol *23,* 146-7, *146-9*

Phoenix, orders of *23, 37,* 145-7; juvenile lodges *23,* 146, *149;* Original Grand Order of the Total Abstinent Sons of 145, *146, 147, 148, 149;* Sisters of the Phoenix *23,* 146; United (Grand) Order of the Total Abstinent Sons of *39,* 145, *148*

Pillars, as symbol 55, 139

Pinkerton Detective Service 53

Pins, tie and lapel *19,* 43, *45*

Poor Law Amendment Act (1834) 14

Primrose League 25, *25*

Processions 16, 18, 22, 27

Prudence: **see** Virtues

Public houses 48-9, *48,* 57, 70, 103

Putney Bridge 43

Quill pen, as symbol 39, *39,* 50, 134, *148*

Rechabites, Order of *37,* 120, 142-5, *142, 143, 144, 145;* tents 143; women in 120

Robes, ceremonial 31, 40, 64, 90, 110, 129

Rose Act 4, 13, 117

Royal Antediluvian Order of Buffaloes: **see** Buffaloes, Royal Antediluvian Order of

Royal Masonic Benevolent Institution 60

Royal Masonic Institution for Boys 60

Royal Masonic Institution for Girls 60

Royal Society 6

St Patrick, Friendly Brothers of 12, *12*

Salamanca, Battle and Lodge of *11*

Samaritan, Parable of the Good, as symbol 52, 122

Sashes 37, 74, 110, 122

Sceptres and maces 43, *141, 146, 147*

Second World War 27, 45, 67, 104

Serpent, as symbol 53, 144

Shepherds, Ancient Order of 94, 124-5, *124, 125, 128;* sanctuaries, 124

Shepherds, Loyal Order of Ancient (Ashton Unity) *29,* 40, *44,* 126-30, *126, 127, 129, 130;* in Scotland 130; Shepherds Friendly Society 127

Skeleton, skull, as symbols: **see** Mortality, emblem of

Slingsby, Henry: **see** Henry Slingsby

Society of Parisians 5

Solomon and Solomon's Temple 54, 57, 62, 85-6

Sons of Israel, Loyal United Lodge of *20*

Sons of Temperance, Order of 149-50, *149*

Stag, as symbol *8,* 9, 122

Stonemasons, stonemasonry 5-6, *59*

Sun, moon and stars, as symbols 54, 139, 144

Sussex, Duke of 62

Sword, used in societies and as symbol 42, 43, 51, 130, 133-6

Tau Delta symbol 43, 112, *112, 113*

Temperance, as symbol: **see** Virtues

Temperance and teetotalism 22, 92, 142-54

Temple, as symbol 55; **see also** Solomon and Solomon's Temple

Tents 143

Time, symbols of 54, 96

Titus, Roman emperor 90

Togo Dubellinus 101-2, *102,* 112

Tolpuddle Martyrs 14, 92

Tools, as symbols *14,* 54-5, 57, 86, *87,* 88-9

Toye, Kenning & Spencer Ltd 29

Trade unions 14-15, *14*

Truro Cathedral *67*

Tutill, George: **see** George Tutill

United Irishmen, Society of 9

United Patriots Friendly Society *13*

United Sisters Friendly Society Suffolk Unity 120

Unity, symbol of 53, 121-2

Unlawful Oaths Act (1797) 9, 14, 92

Unlawful Societies Act (1789) 9, 13, 14, 92, 102

Virtues, as symbols *7,* 51-2, 133-6, 139, 141, *152*

Wands, as symbol 51

Water Rats 25, *25*

West Indies 84, 95

Whitsun 18, 22

Women in friendly and fraternal societies 4, 21-2, *23,* 25, 49, *68,* 68-9, 76, 95, 120-1, 146, 153

Zodiac, as symbol 54, 113